DARK CITY

DAMIANI

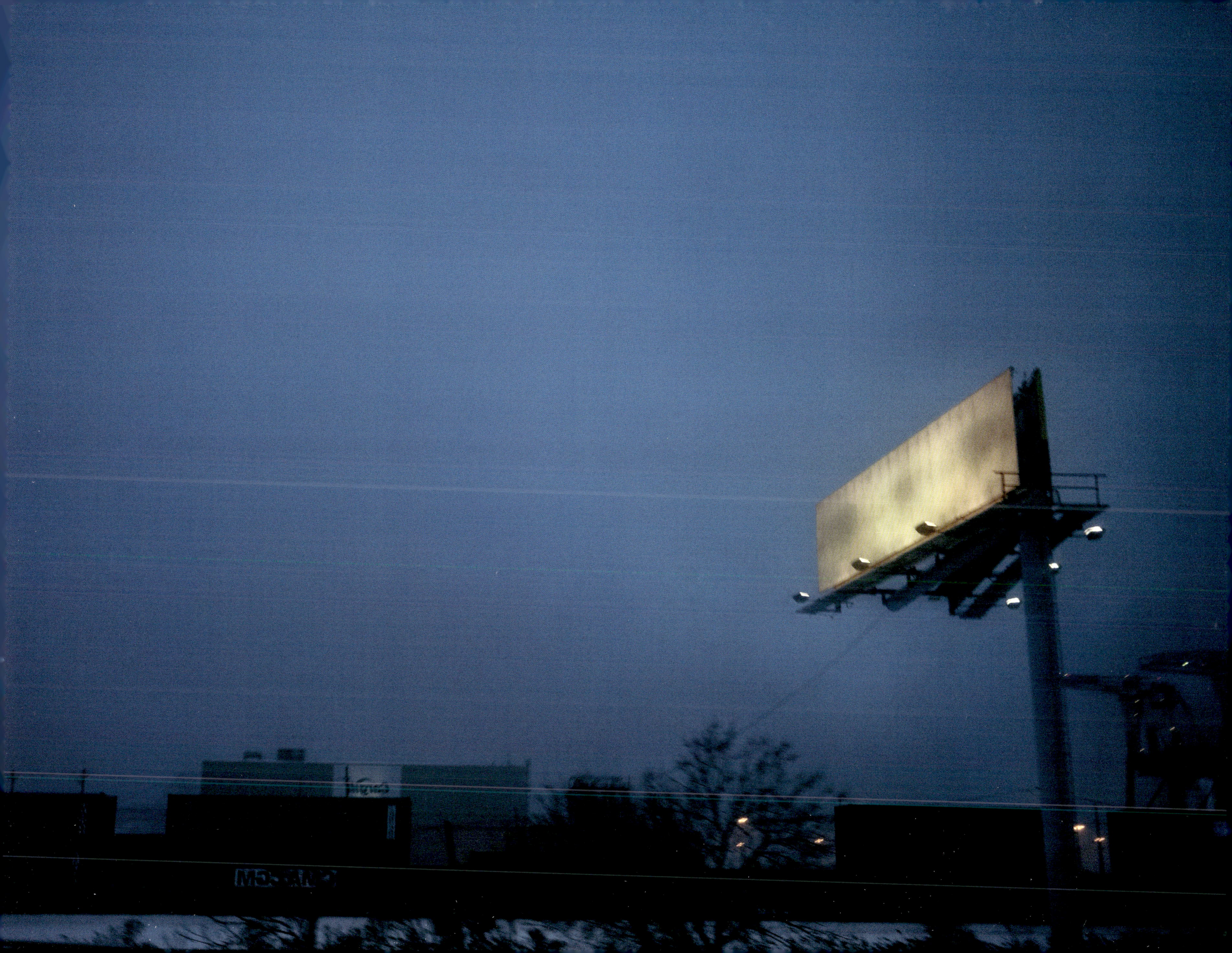

LYNN SAVILLE

DARK CITY

Pages 2–3: Blank Billboard, I-95, Baltimore, Maryland

Abandoned Michigan Central Depot, Detroit, Michigan

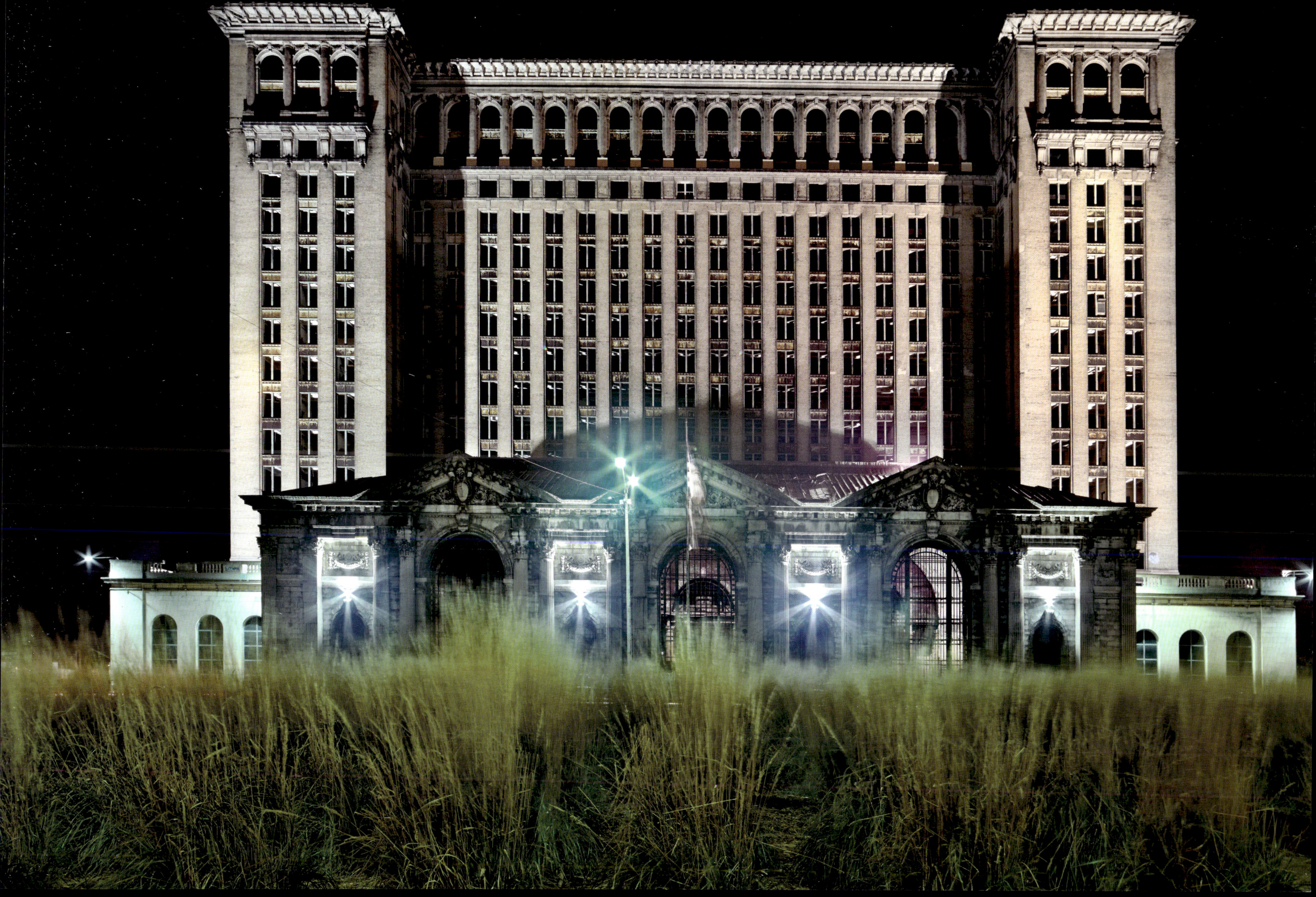

THE ARCHAEOLOGY OF OVERNIGHT

Toward the end of her life Diane Arbus said that she had come to "love what I can't see in a photograph. In Brassaï, in Bill Brandt, there is the element of actual physical darkness and it's very thrilling to see darkness again." Thrilling but risky. Responding somewhat dismissively to William Gedney's proposed series "The Night," John Szarkowski, head of photography at the Museum of Modern Art in New York, commented that photography is about what you *can* see, whereas these were about what you could not see. The dilemma is as simple as it is complex: to allow us to see that which cannot be seen. Hence the attraction of twilight or dusk when the seen is poised to disappear into the unseen, when the daylight world of facts begins subtly to slide into the realm of dreams. While the overall mood will always be tinged with romance, the atmosphere of a given picture depends on *how* dark it is, on the balance between memory—of the day that has gone—and the promise of what the night will bring. At dawn the dreams of night give way to the facts of day, when you are able to see what was previously hidden.

Lynn Saville has wandered purposefully through every phase of the nocturnal world, from dusk through deep night to dawn. As a photographer, daylight seems to hold roughly the same attraction for her that it does for a vampire. It is as if, in developing such finely calibrated night vision, the capacity for seeing in broad daylight has been correspondingly diminished.

Between twilight or daybreak lie the variously extended vacancies between places falling into disuse (and out of sight) and being refitted and reseen (with the shared word, *shutter*, uniting premises and camera). Throughout *Dark City*, in other words, we see the economic equivalent of the diurnal cycle of night and day, light and dark. Much economic planning is dedicated to breaking this cycle whereby bust follows boom as surely as night follows day. Unapologetic advocates of the free market claim that each bust creates the conditions for a more splendid boom. Either way, on a daily or nightly basis, in cities all over the world, we witness this cycle of closing down and opening up: the seasonal shifts of capital as places go out of business because of rent hikes (during times of prosperity) or bankruptcy (during a recession) before falling into disuse for a while (brief in periods of prosperity, extended in a recession) before being reborn either as cafés, pop-ups, or (less happily) as "Everything for a Dollar" stores. In reality, it's all more complicated than that, of course. Some streets undergo such a boom that there are always empty premises because rents are rising so quickly that fashionable new businesses succumb to the same fate as the quaintly outmoded ones they have displaced. So the boom is adorned and littered with evidence of bust. Residents view these periods of transition with the vested interest of people anxiously awaiting news of a family member who is in hospital: will the outcome be recovery or further decline? In the hopeful meantime, a vacated site becomes a place of intense employment as architects, construction workers, designers, and fitters prepare for its new life . . . as a café, a restaurant, or whatever it's going to be. And so the empty site becomes pregnant with meaning.

While the same forces—economic, planetary—converge on many images and places in this book, they are observed formally rather than didactically. Saville

BY GEOFF DYER

is fascinated by conflicting colors, reflections, and forms of illumination (street lamps, floods, neon, fluorescent strips) and how they interact and react, not so much to being seen, but to being filmed.

There is something lovely about the fall, when twilight coincides with people coming out of offices, as the working day gives way to the leisure and romance—well, the drinking at any rate—of evening. And then there are those extended summer days when twilight falls shortly before people head home to sleep. Saville, however, is relatively uninterested in these interludes of heavy foot traffic. Part of the appeal of the night, for her, is that densely populated areas become largely unpeopled. At night a reclamation seems to take place. It's not that the city becomes uninhabited; more that it is inhabited by itself, by premises and windows, walls and doors, all of which seem to exist for their own sakes, not as conduits to or components of social interaction. This is signalled by the very first picture, of a blank billboard on the road in Baltimore: a lyrical declaration that the journey to be undertaken in these pages is to a city or destination stripped of many of its usual attractions and functions. The neon SPACE FOR RENT sign on West 51st Street in New York advertises its own emptiness so effectively that it seems a shame to convert it to any other use. A string of lights takes on the appearance of an after-hours art installation at—the opposite of a gallery opening—a *closing*. Occasionally there is evidence of what might be called the archaeology of overnight: resting tools, tired steps, dreaming brooms, sleeping shadows. The occasional human presence serves not to diminish

but to enhance the sense of emptiness, to bear witness to sites of vacant self-sufficiency without disturbing or intruding on them.

With our attention fixed on what is before our eyes—no urge to look behind, over our shoulders—these nights, these places, are entirely without fear. They give us a sense of being invisible. And so a strange inversion takes place. The night becomes visible as we fade from sight. We are represented either by token figures, their reflections, or by a shadow (the photographer's own), deepening the impression that it is the buildings, the doors and windows—the lighted night itself—doing the looking. This is Neighborhood Watch in pure, unthreatened form.

The clarity of seeing also makes us conscious of the silence—which is absolute. There is no rumble of traffic or of subterranean bass from night clubs, no dawn chorus even. The pristine silence, the lack of motion in these very still photographs, create the sense of a world that has dropped out of time— and therefore out of the cycle of transactions. Stripped of contemporary merchandise and tell-tale signage, empty premises become difficult to date so that they seem sometimes to have dropped not only out of time but of *history*. And yet, at the same time, so to speak, we are conscious in many of them that this is a transitory or fleeting phenomenon. Instead of a world that has dropped out of time, then, we should more accurately speak of instants that have dropped out of time. Hence the tension in images in which there is a conspicuous lack of drama or tension. The vacancy is both spatial and temporal   and *Dark City* is full of it.

"

String of Lights, Harlem, New York City

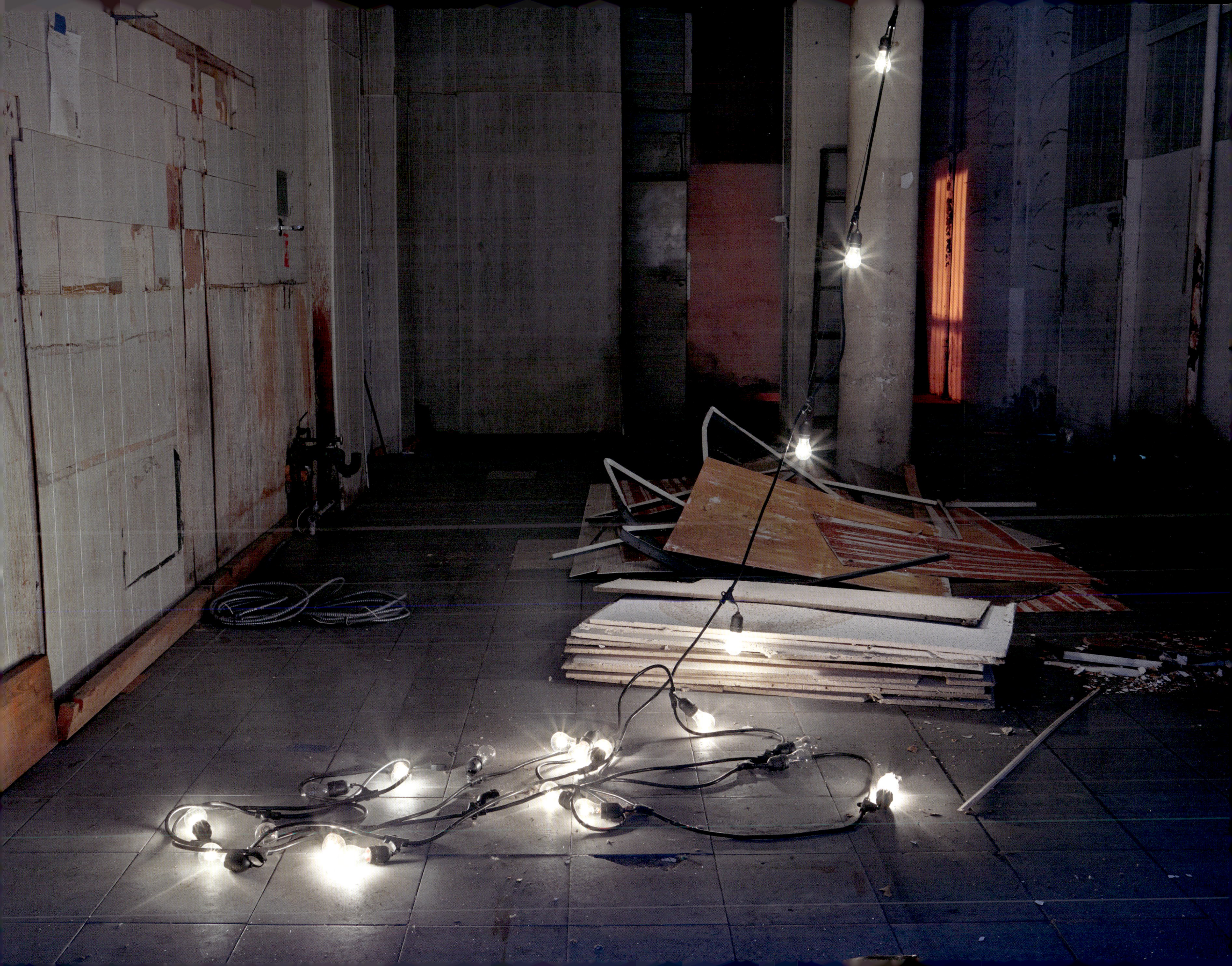

Brooklyn Bridge Park Construction, Brooklyn, New York

Page 14: Greenpoint Warehouse, Brooklyn, New York

Page 15: Tribal Techno, Madison Avenue, New York City

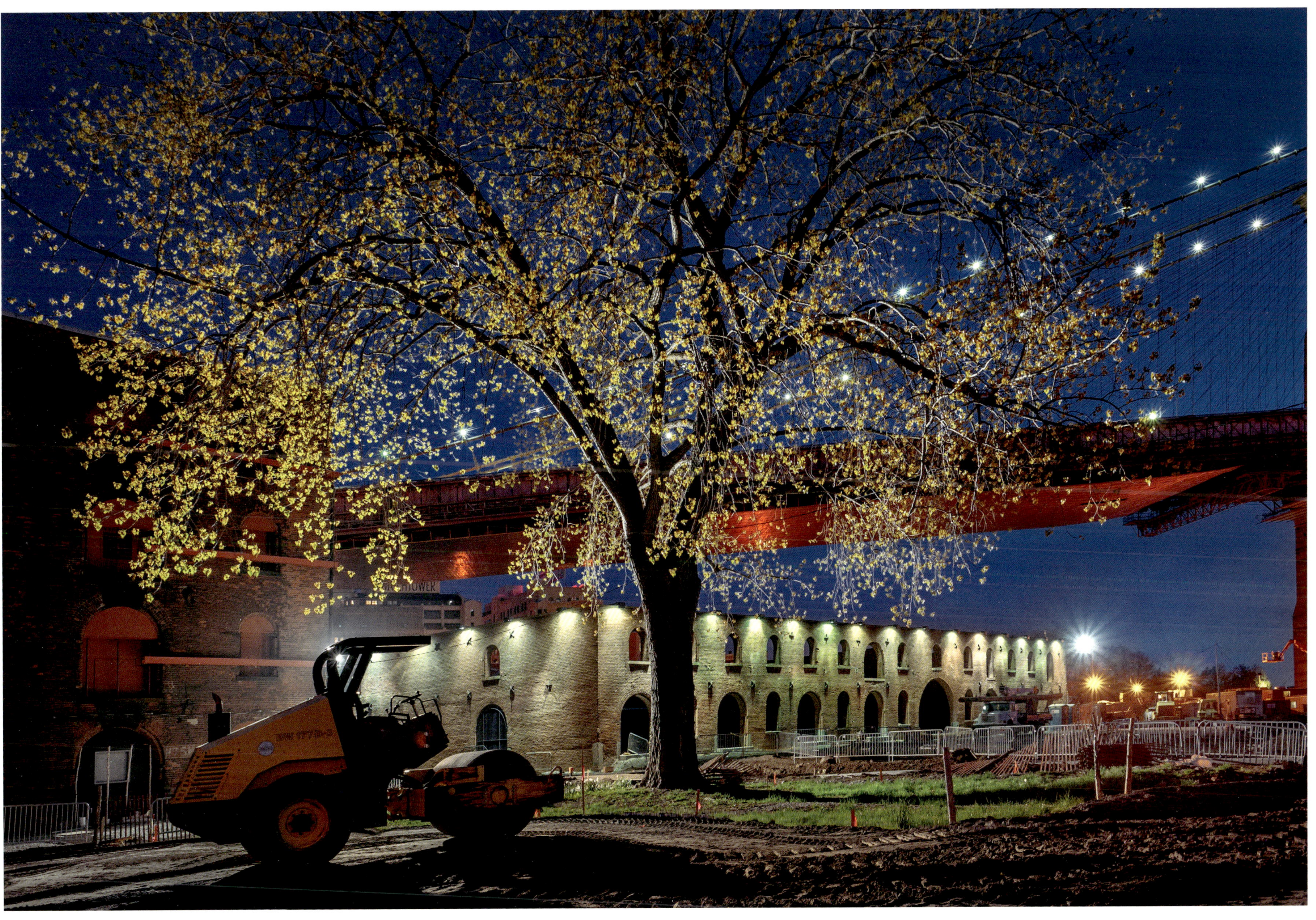

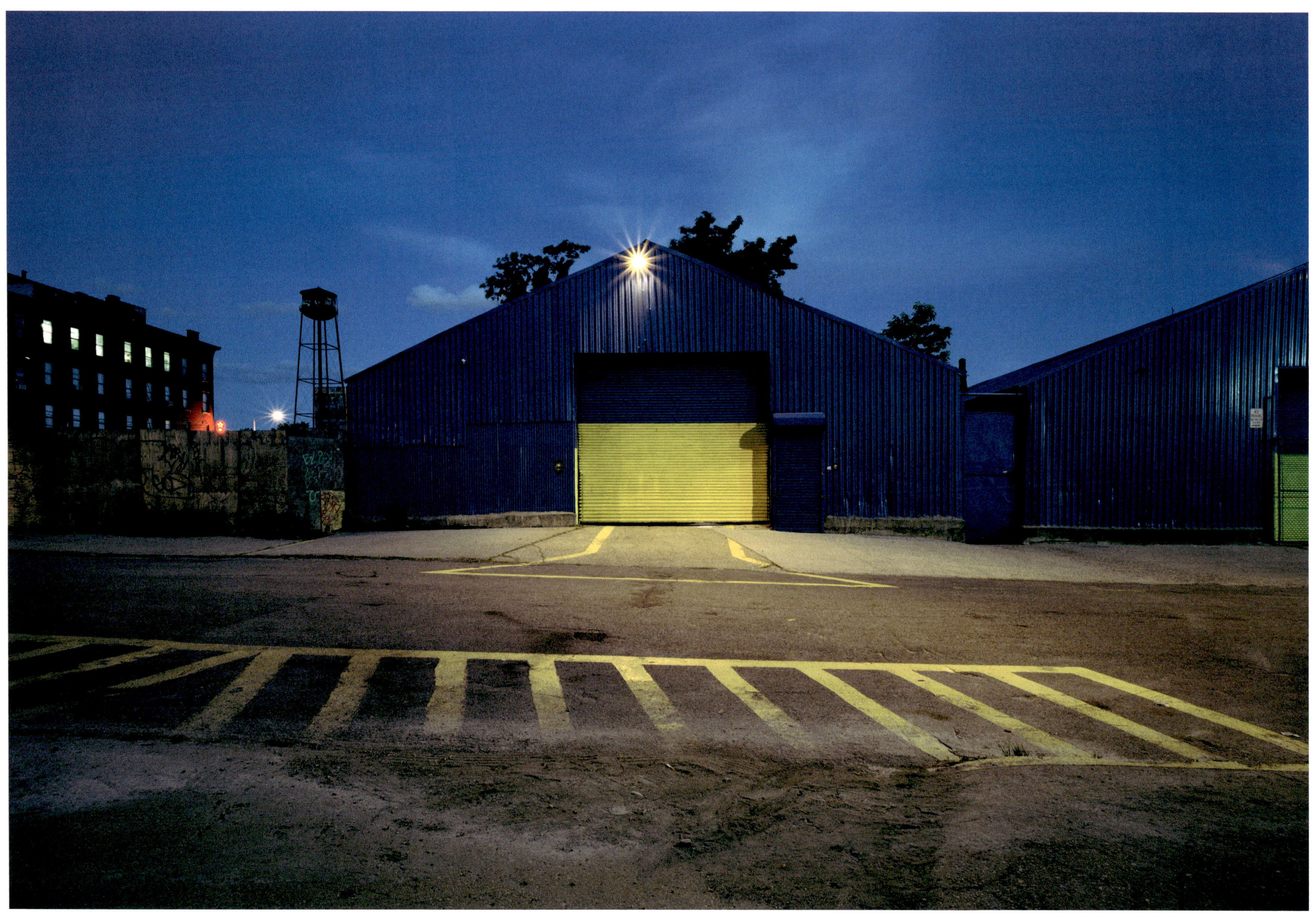

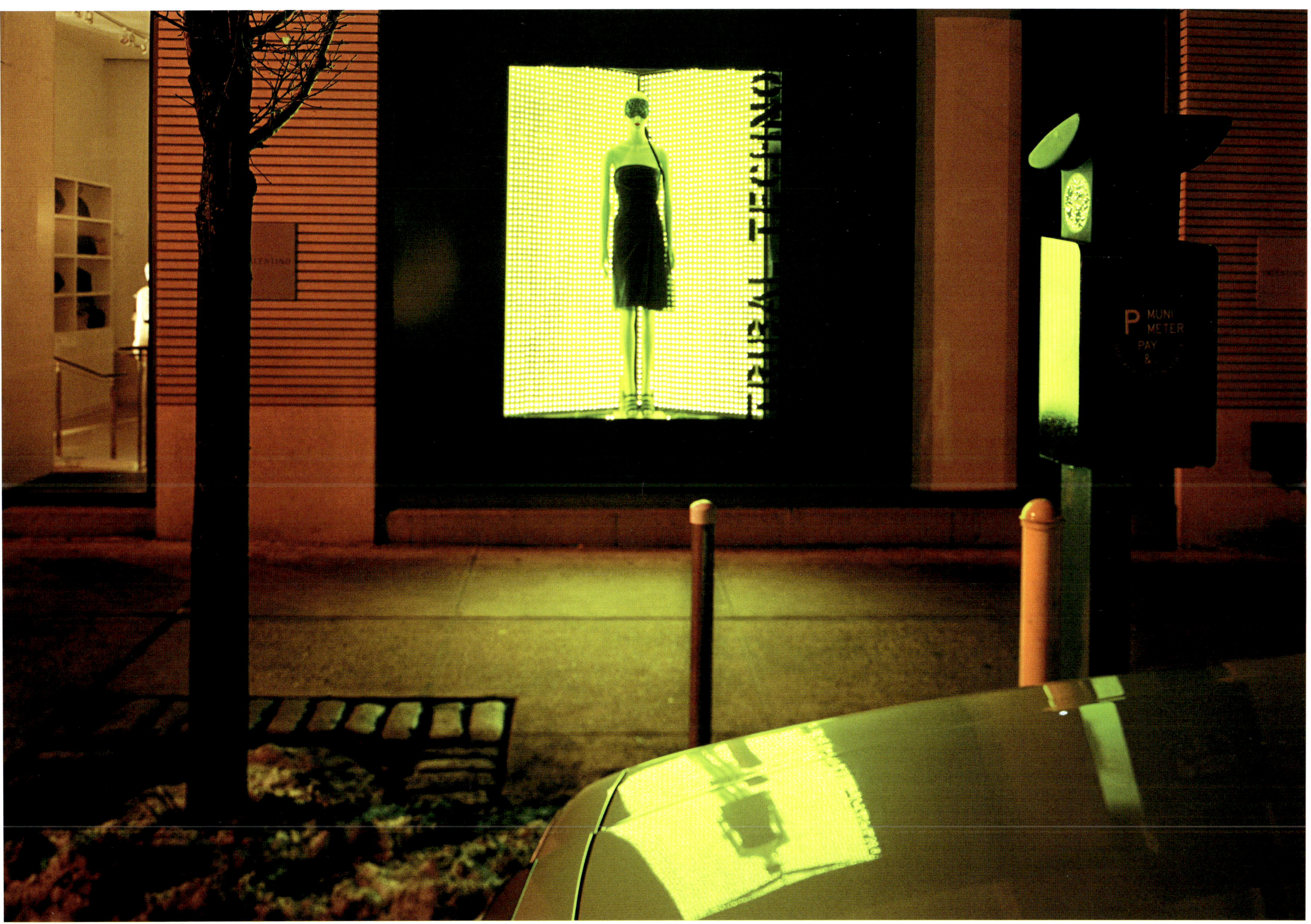
VALENTINO
VALENTINO
P
MUNI
METER
PAY
&

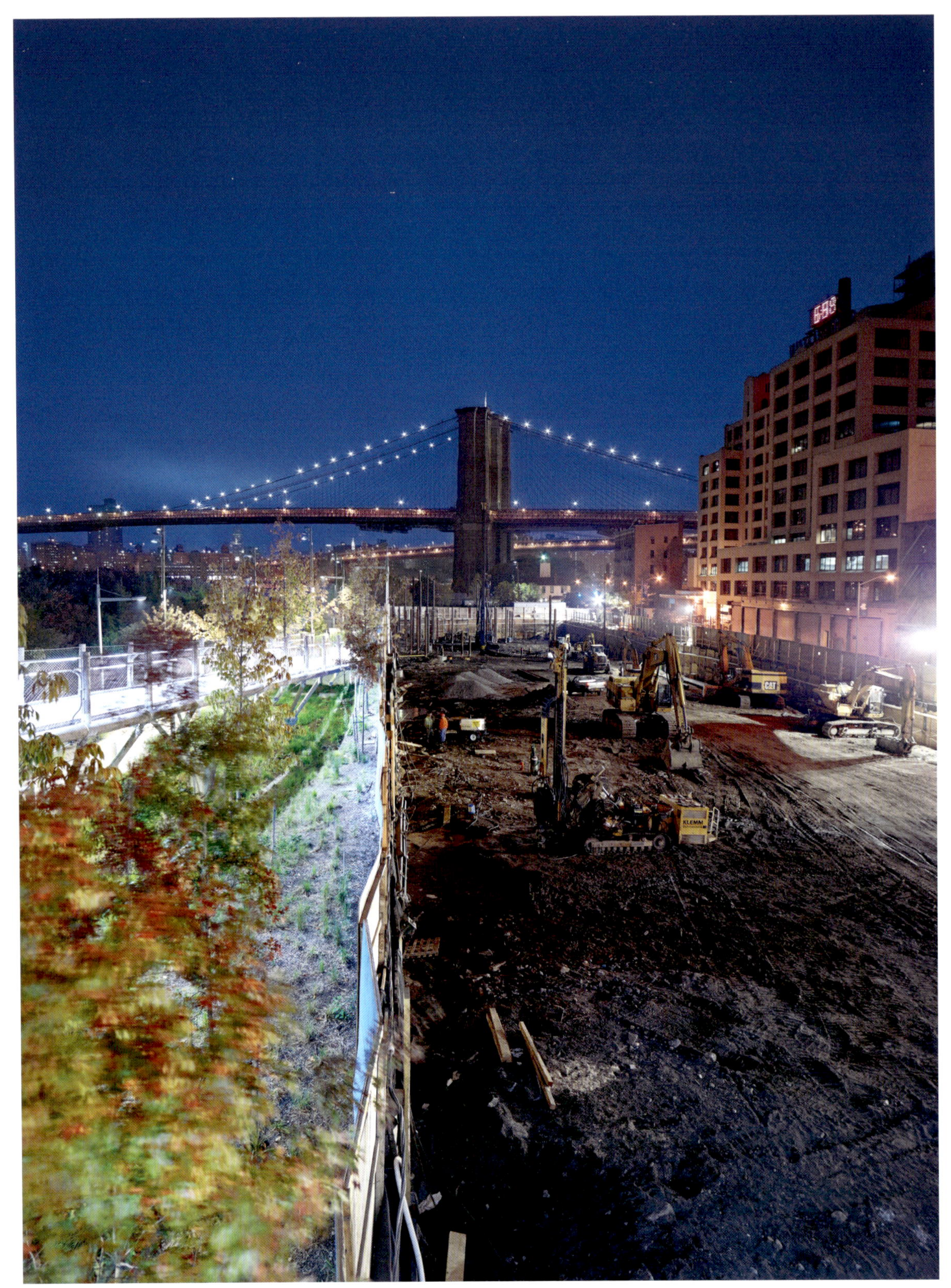

Fulton Ferry Landing Park
from Footbridge, Brooklyn, New York

Opposite: Girl on the High Line,
New York City

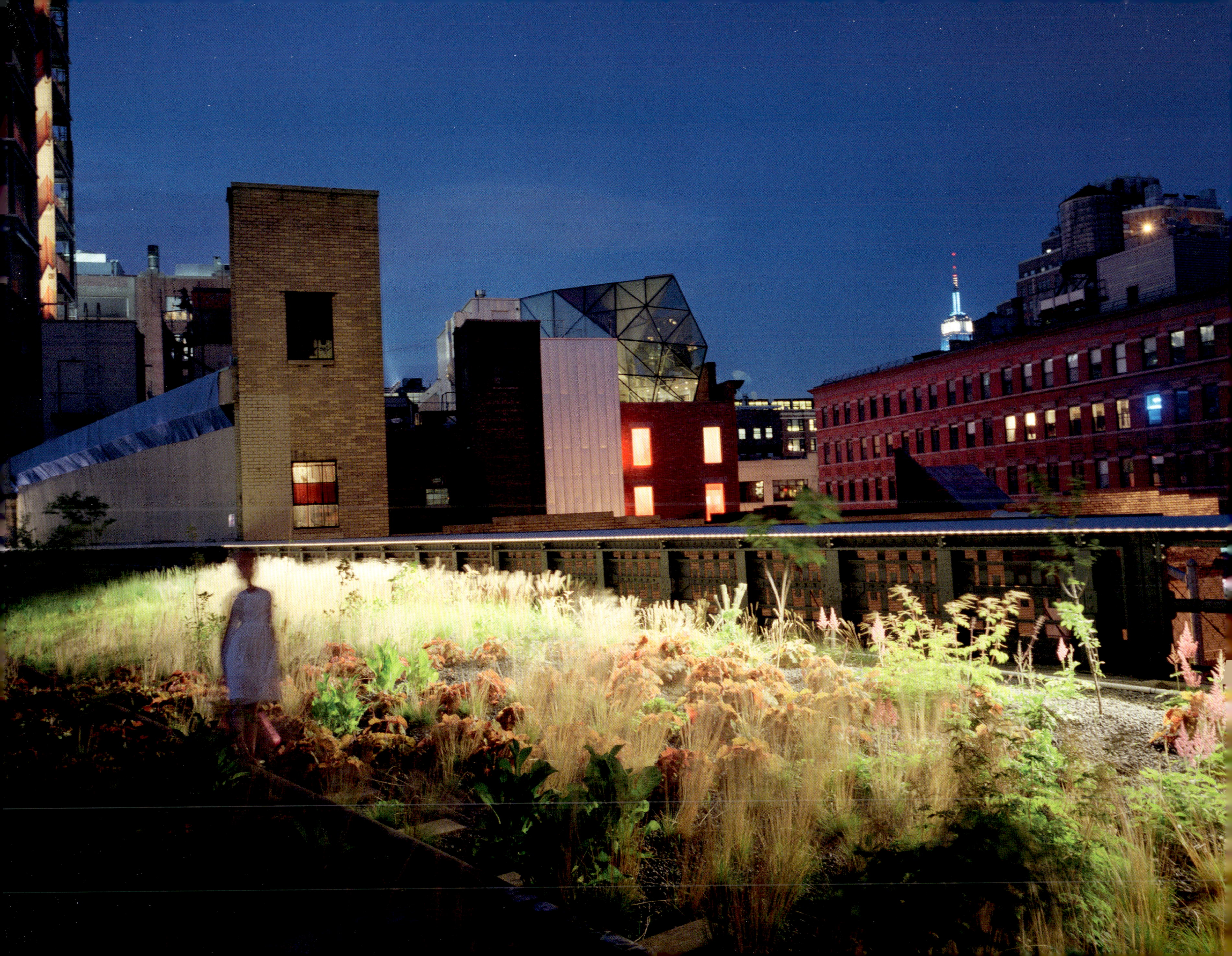

Corner Store, Beverly Hills, California

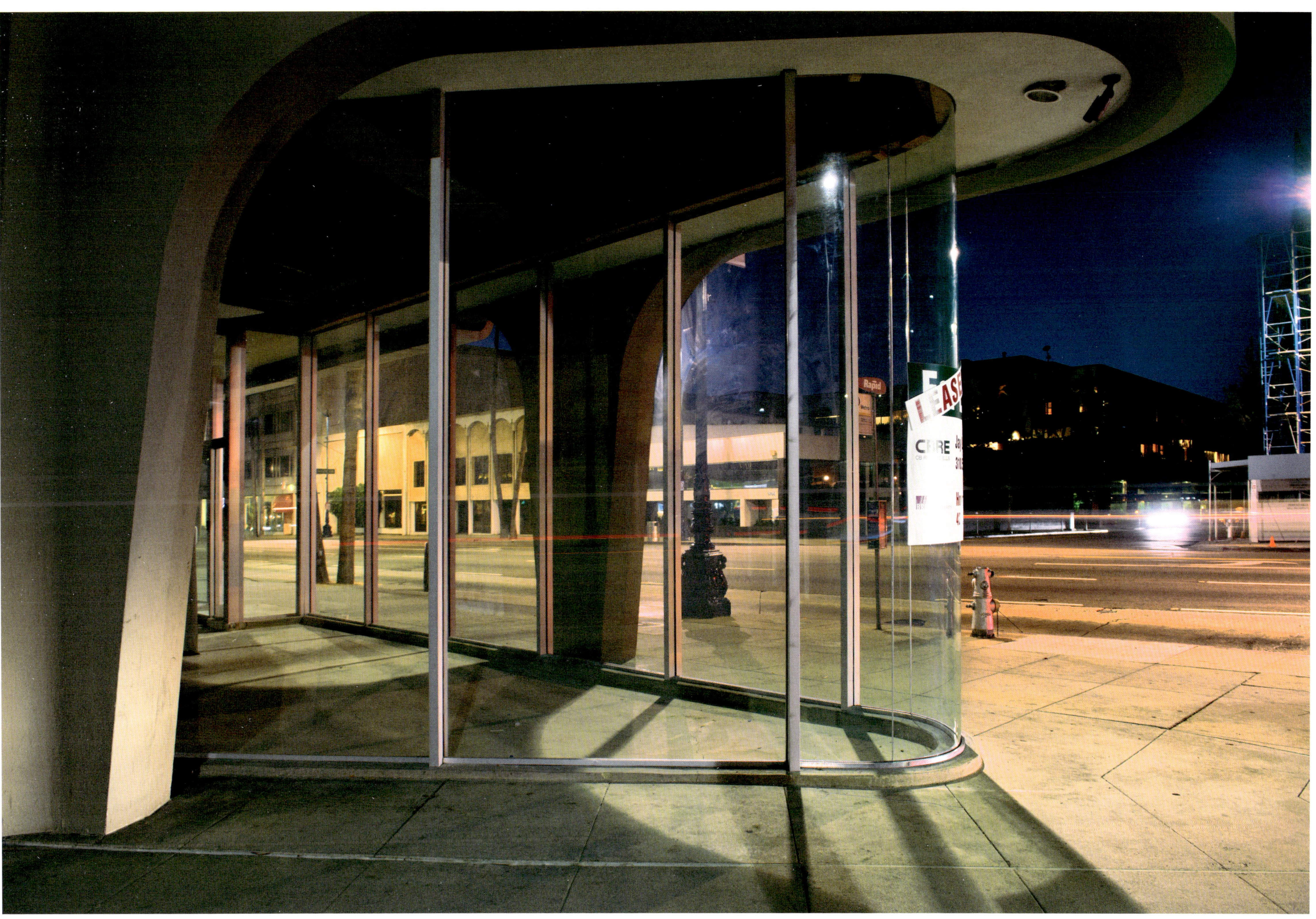

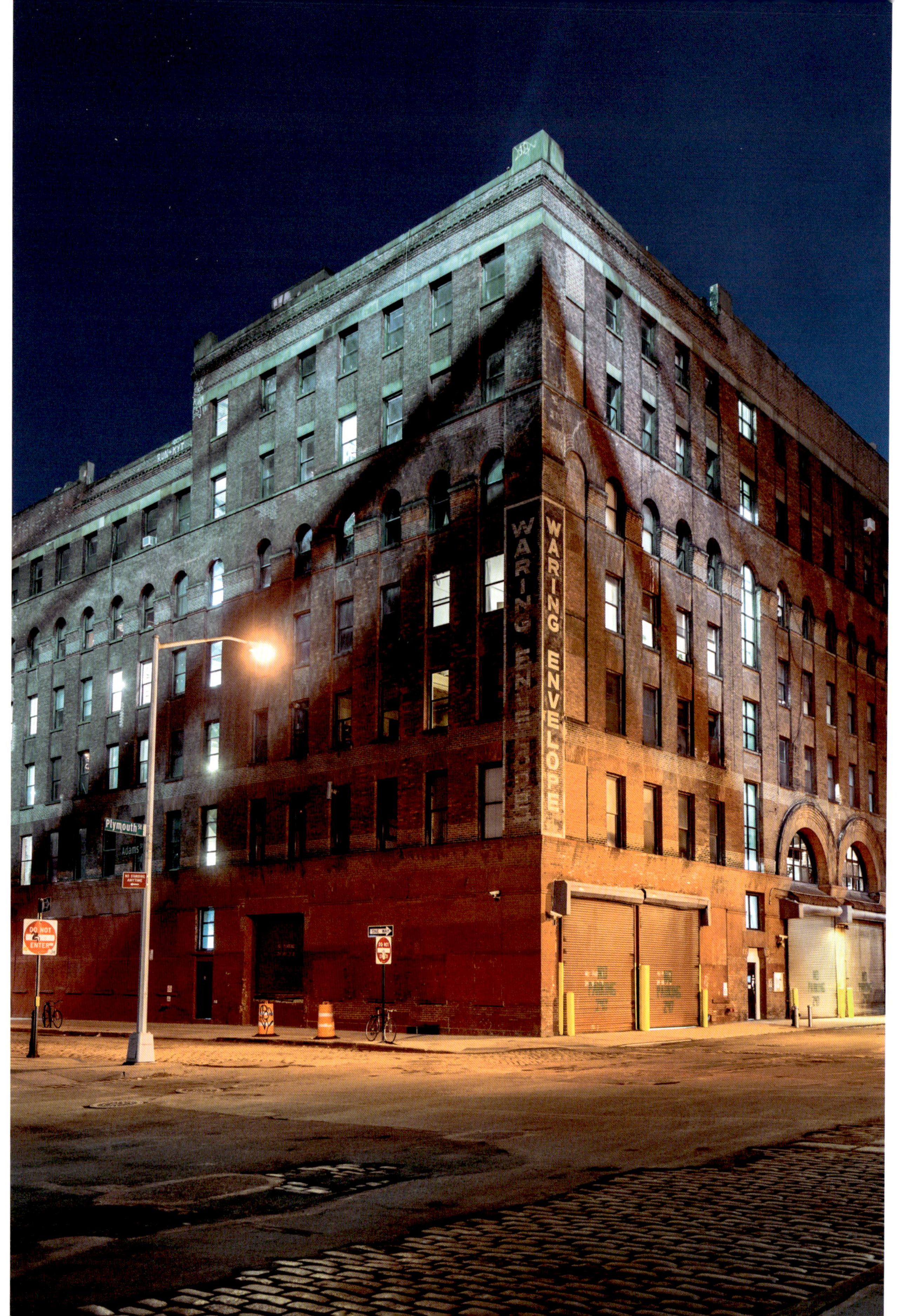

Waring Envelope Warehouse,
Brooklyn, New York

Opposite: Parking Lot,
Houston, Texas

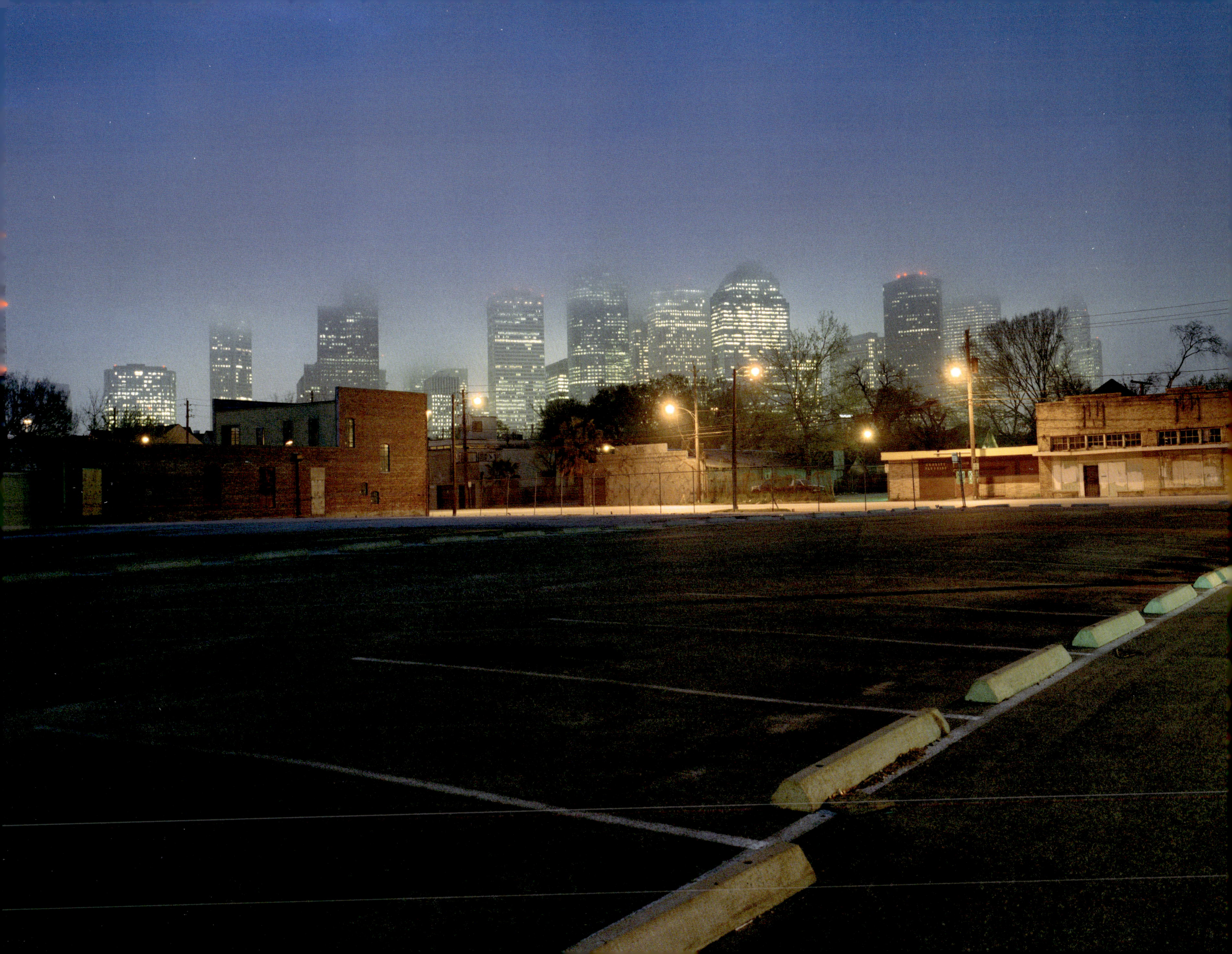

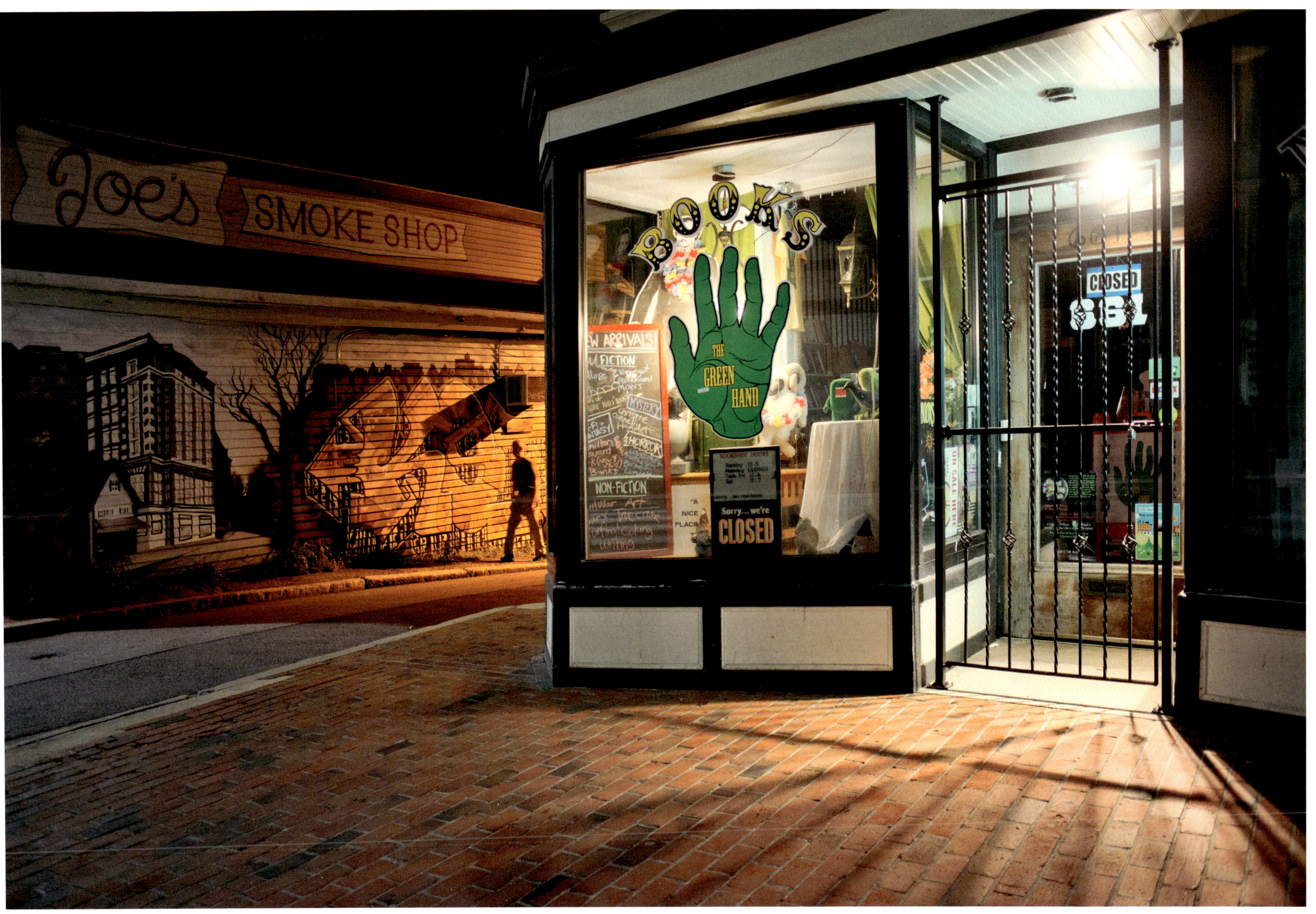
Joe's
SMOKE SHOP
BOOKS
THE GREEN HAND
NEW ARRIVALS!
FICTION
MYSTERY
HORROR
NON-FICTION
CLOSED
Sorry... we're
CLOSED

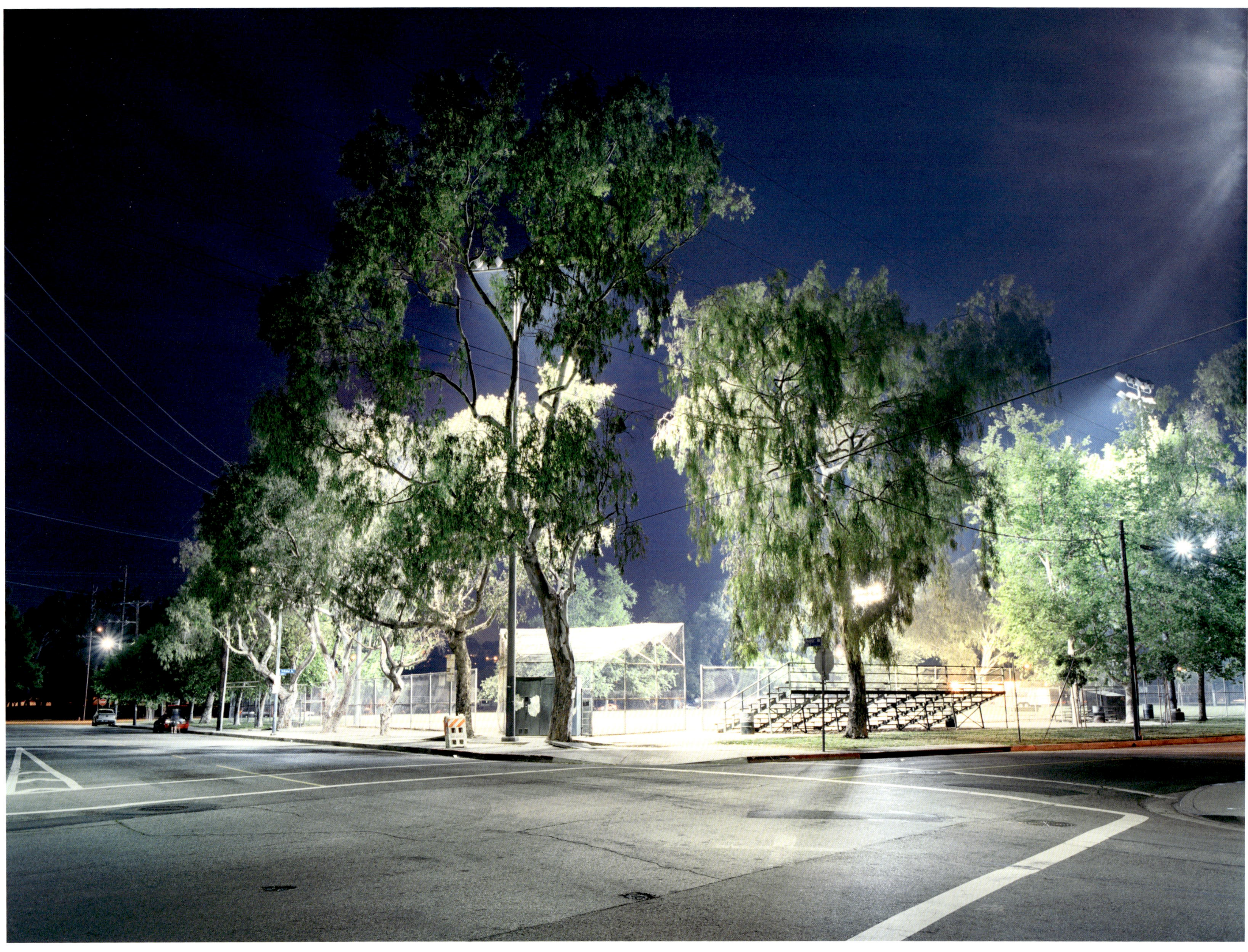

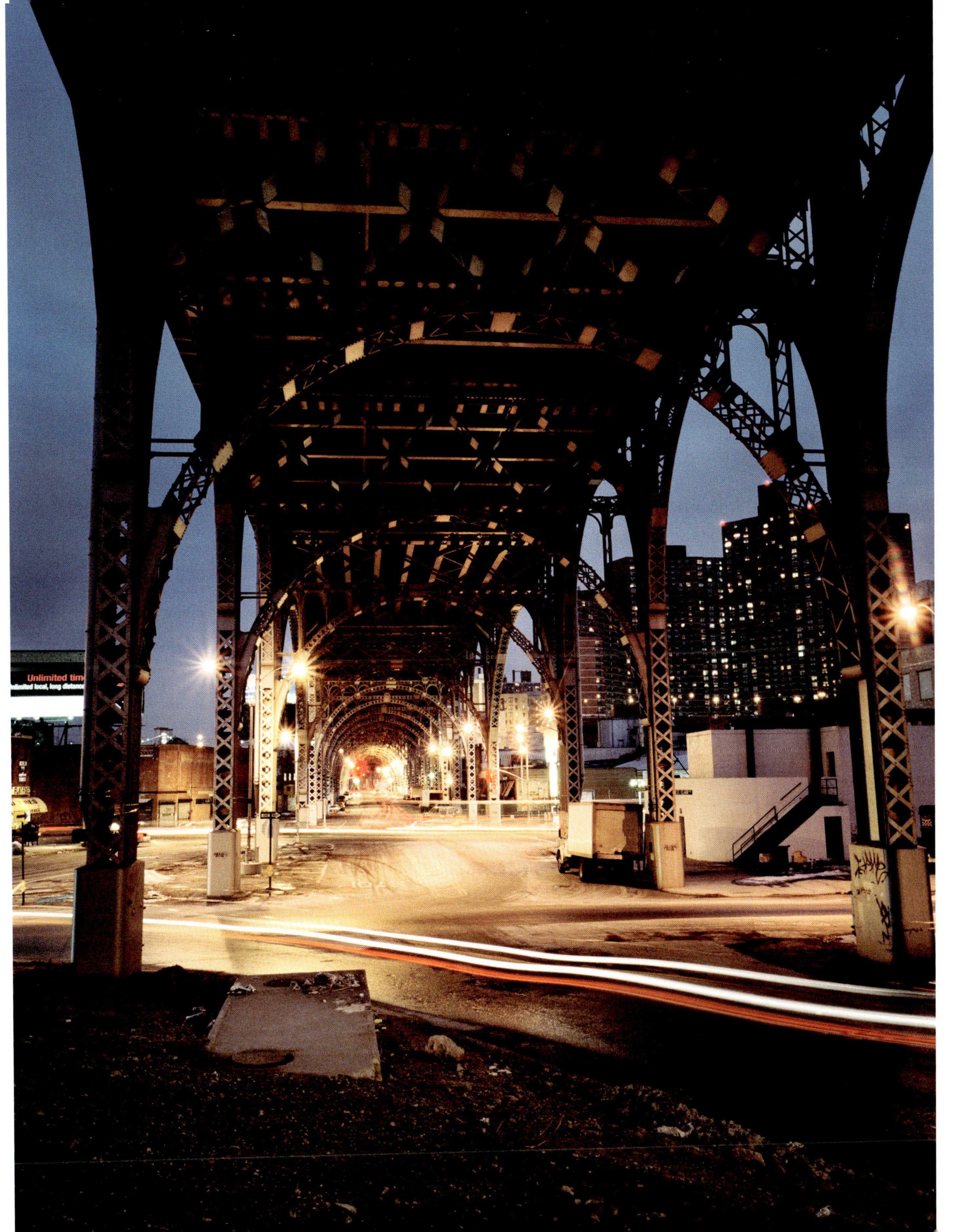

Opposite: Baseball Field,
Venice, California

Viaduct, West 125th Street,
New York City

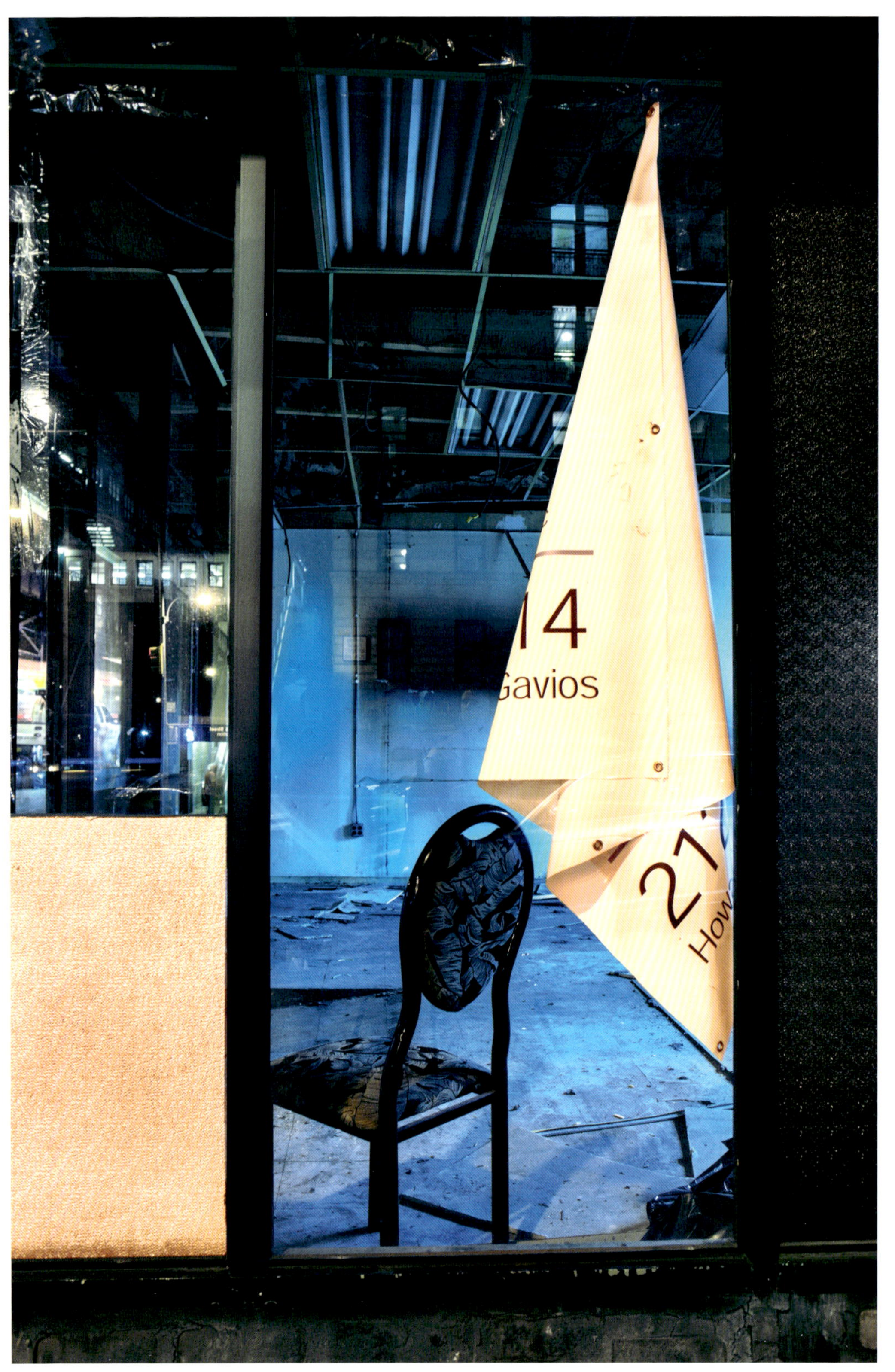

Tiemann Place, New York City

Opposite: Underpass Mural, Albany, New York

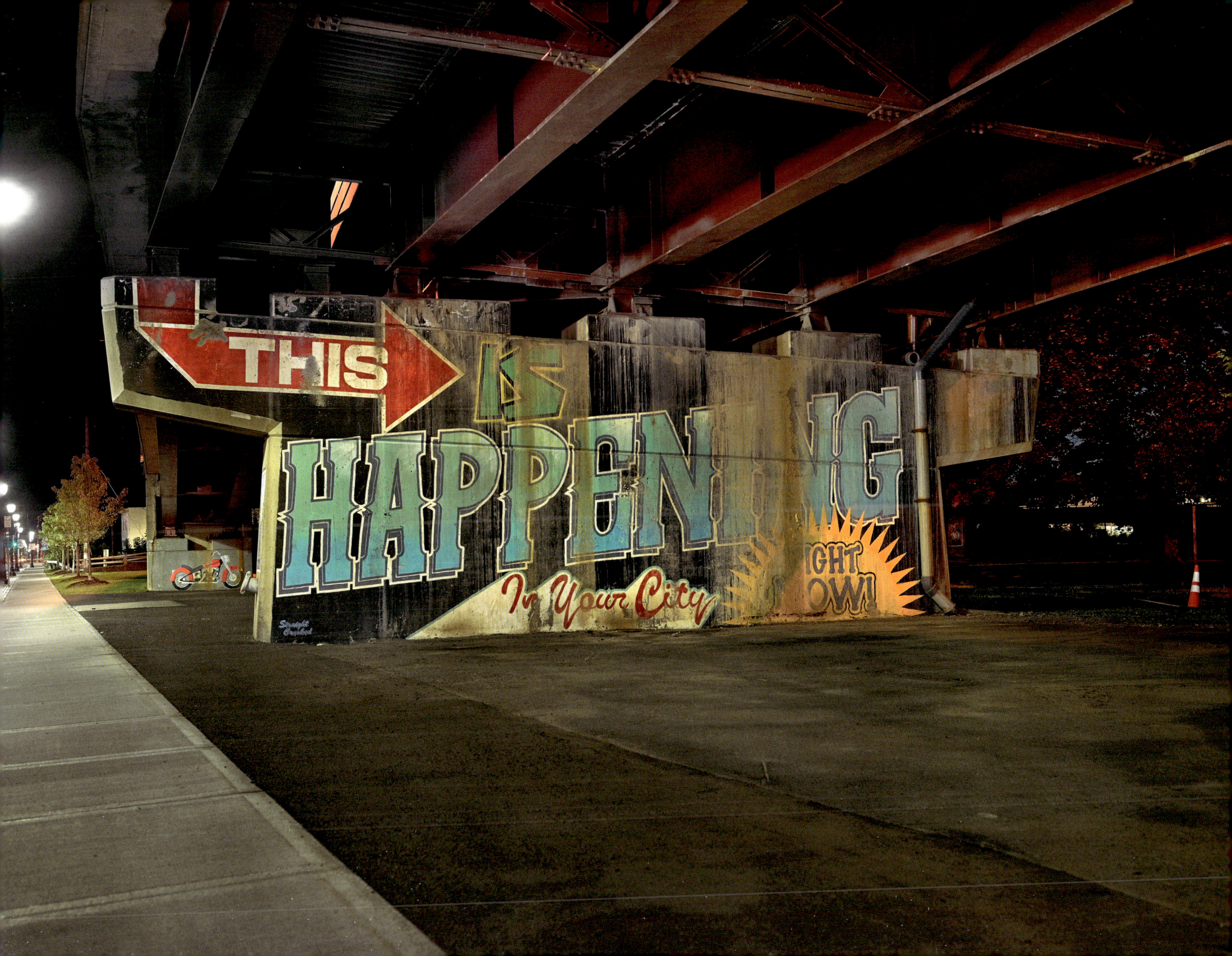

THIS
IS
HAPPENING
In Your City
RIGHT NOW!
Straight Crooked

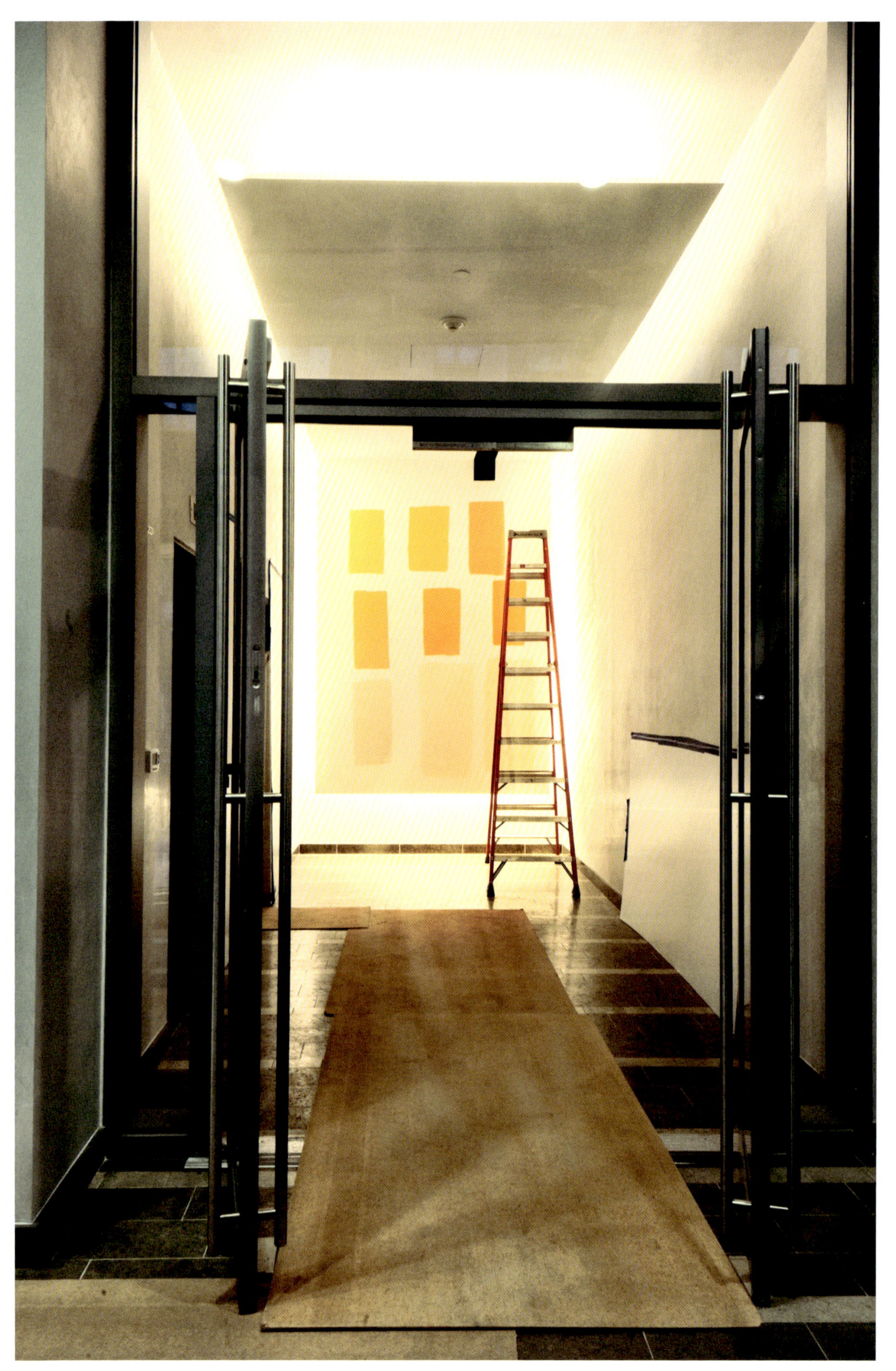

Lobby, Amsterdam Avenue, New York City

Opposite: Warehouse, Chicago, Illinois

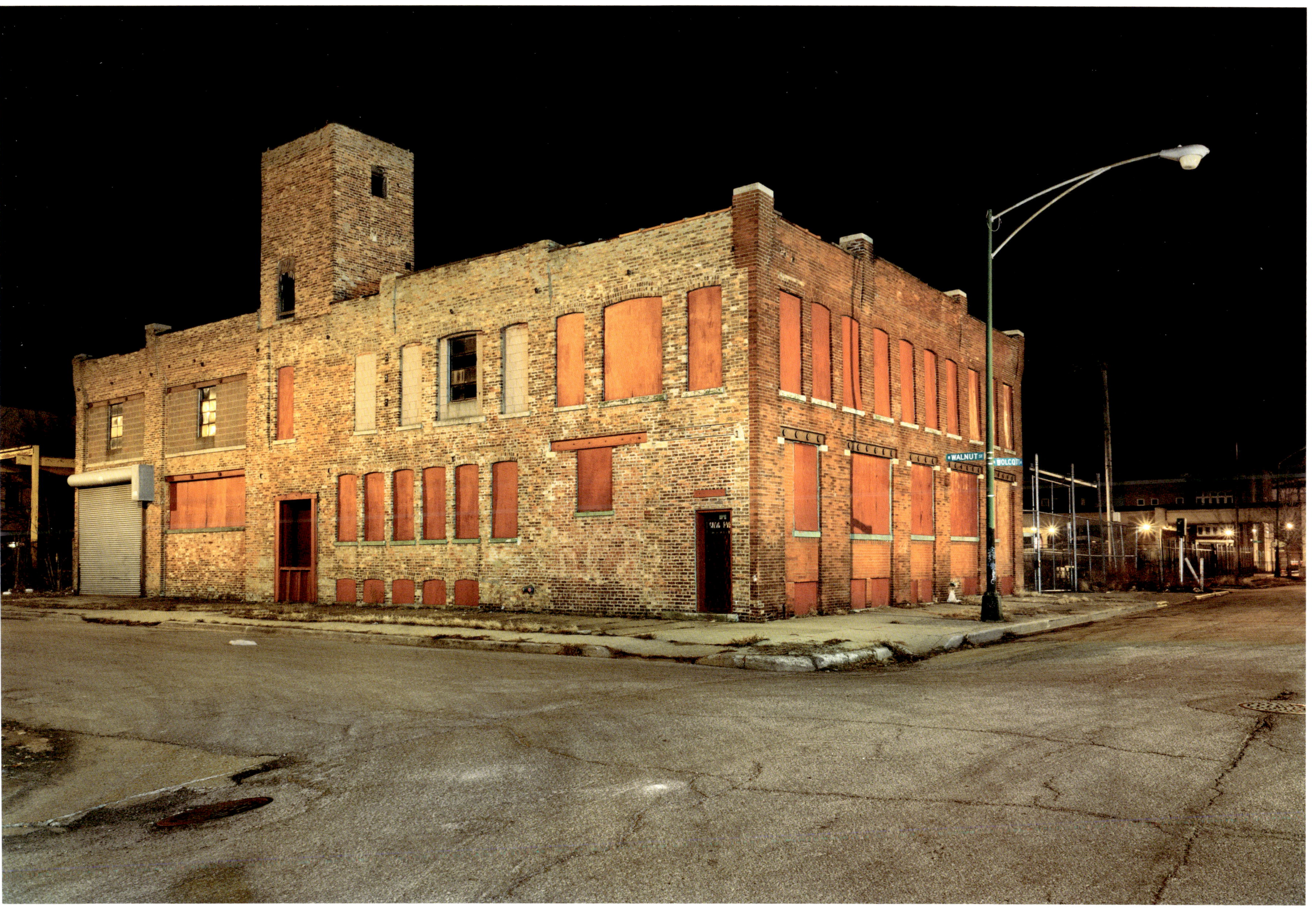

WALNUT ST
WOLCOTT

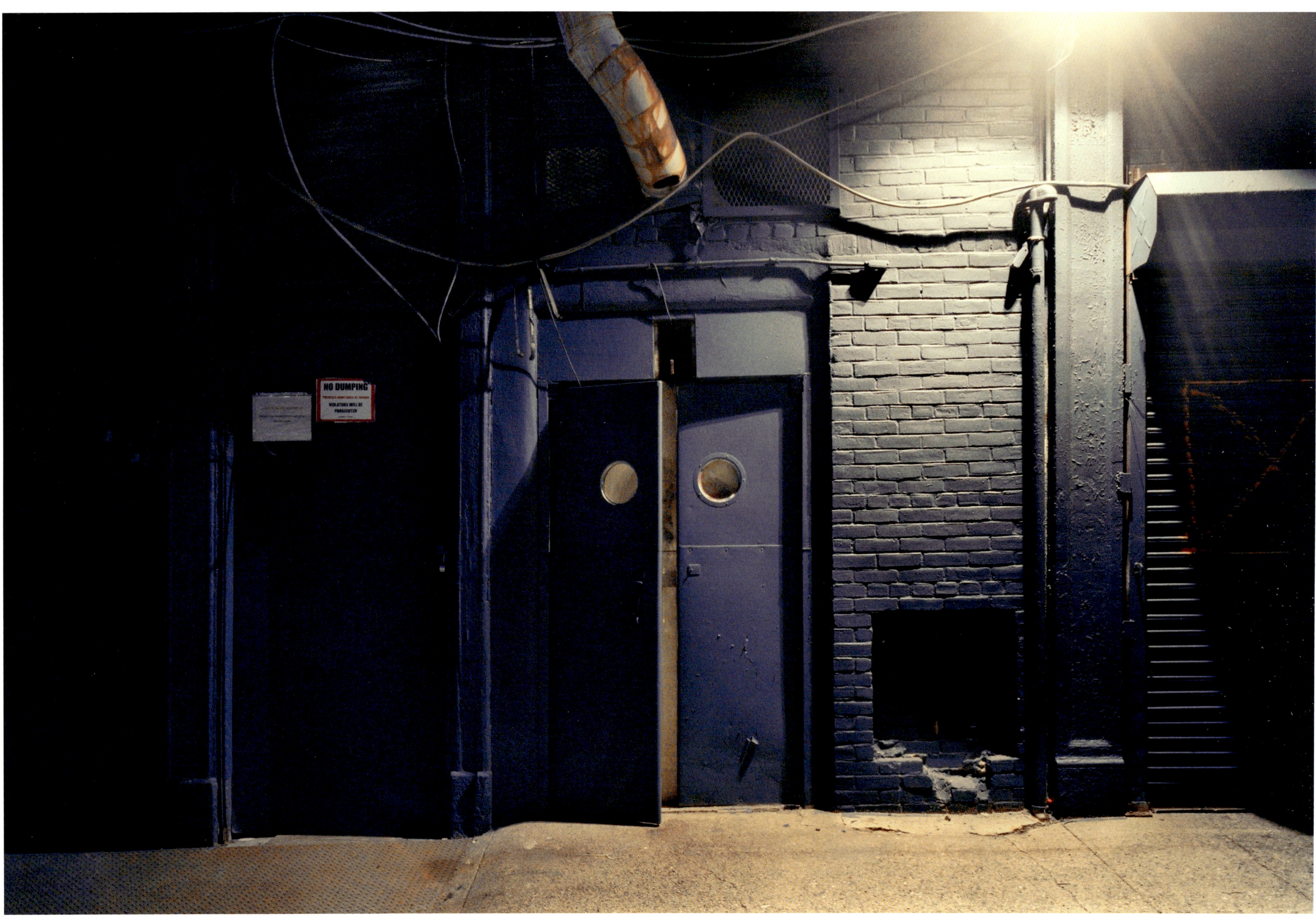
NO DUMPING
VIOLATORS WILL BE
PROSECUTED

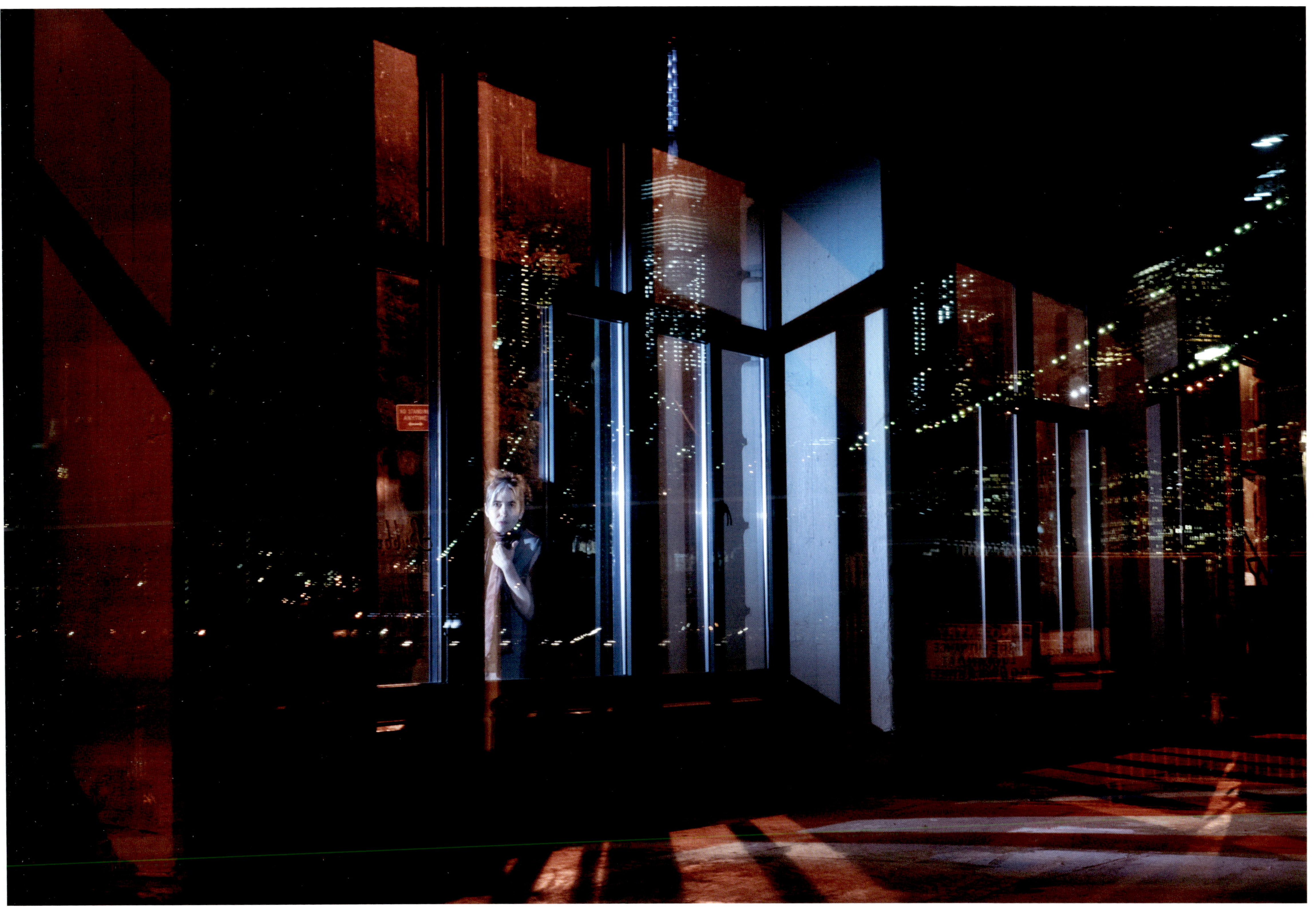

Page 30: Meatpacking District, New York City

Page 31: Main Street, Brooklyn, New York

Neon Sign, West 50th Street, New York City

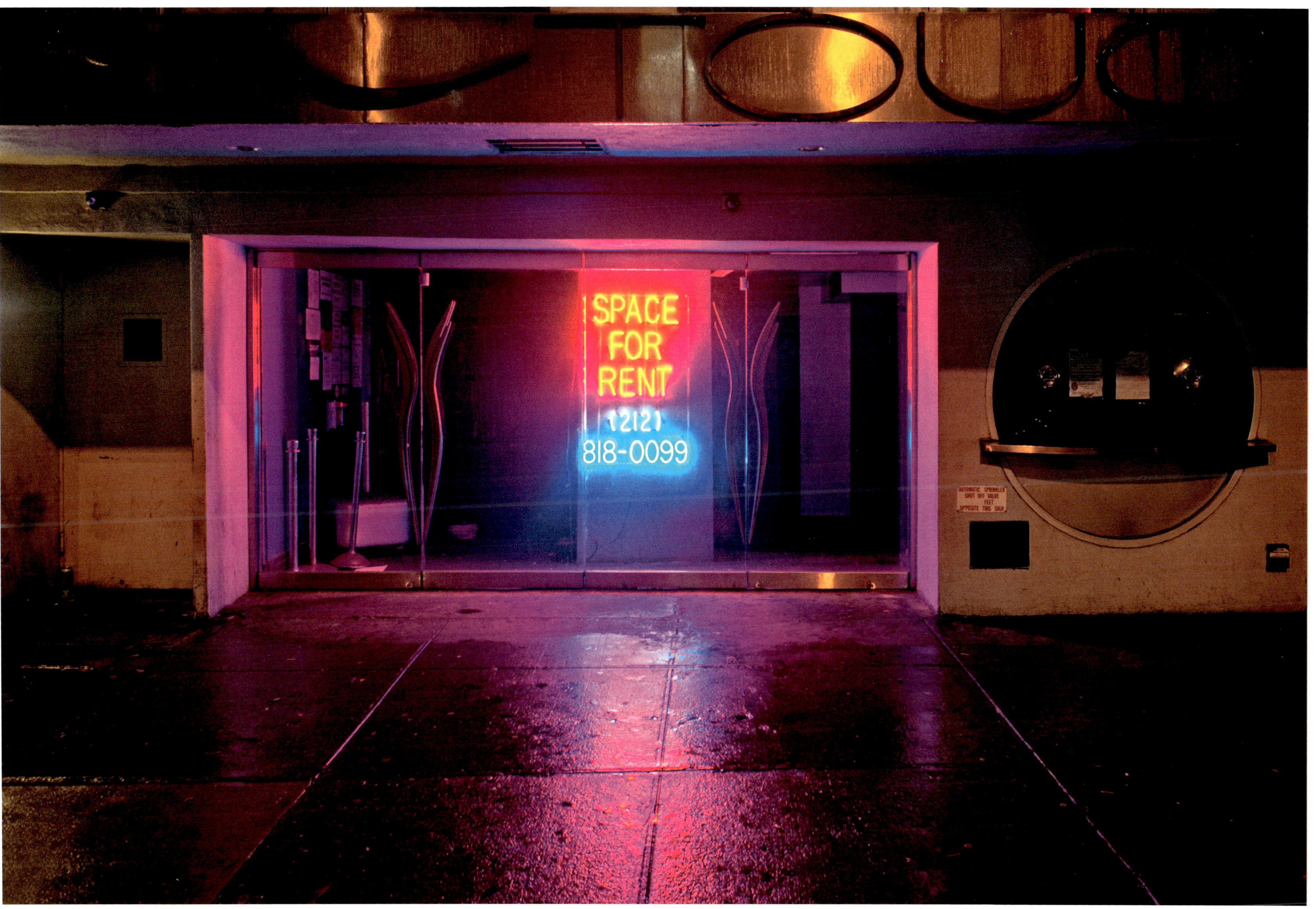
SPACE
FOR
RENT
(212)
818-0099

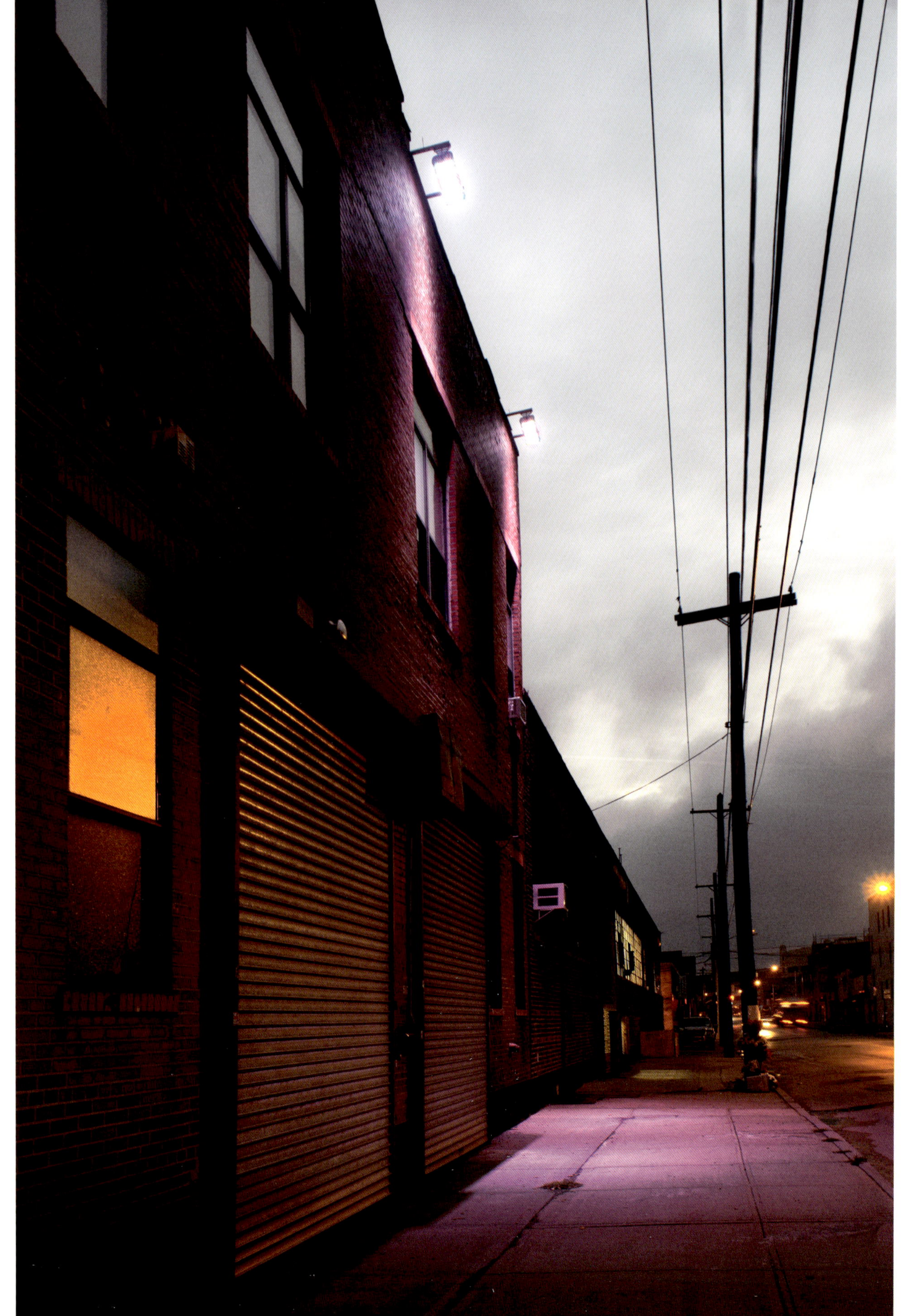

Warehouses, Bushwick, Brooklyn, New York

Opposite: Empty Gallery, Chelsea, New York

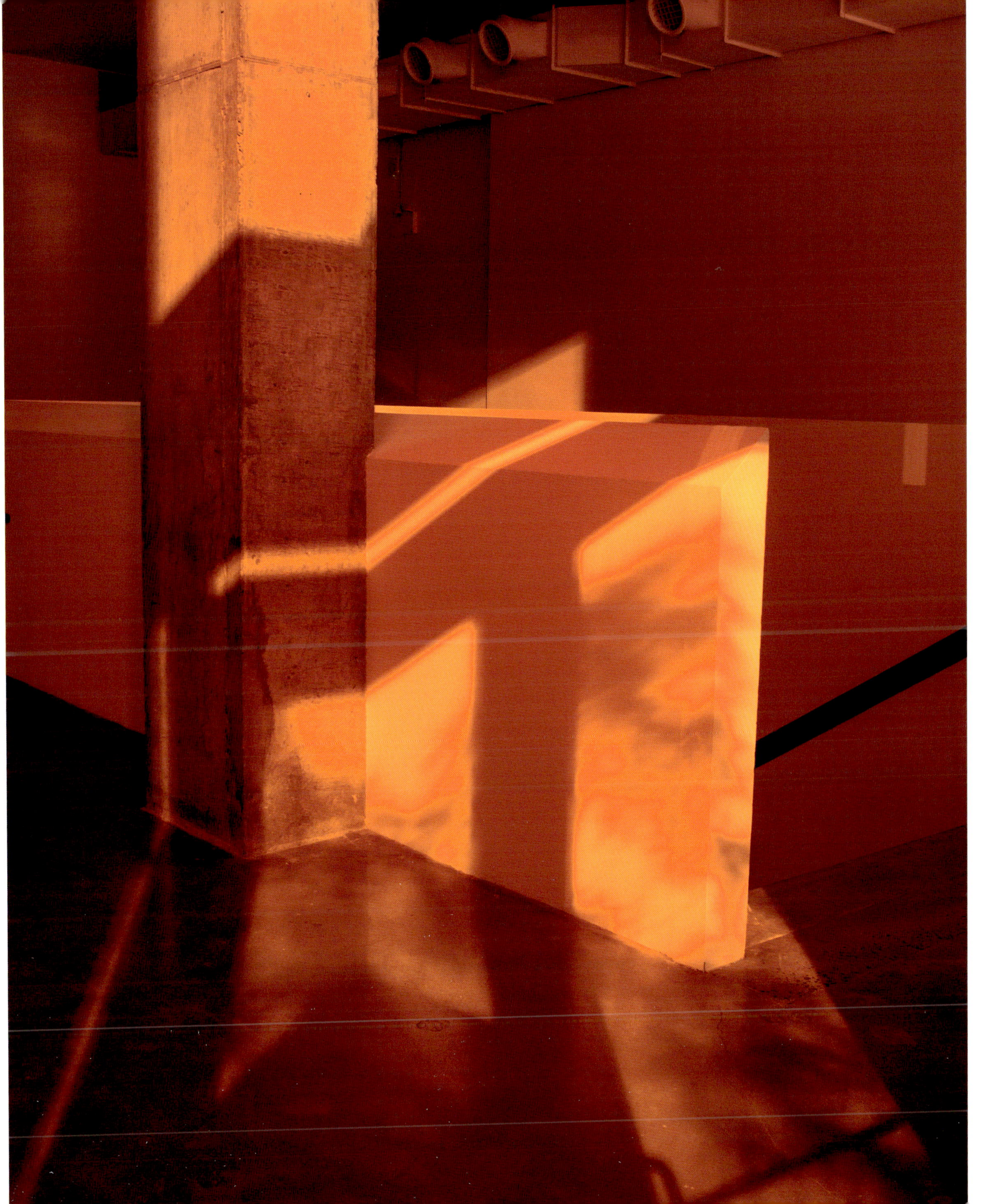

Columbia University Construction, New York City

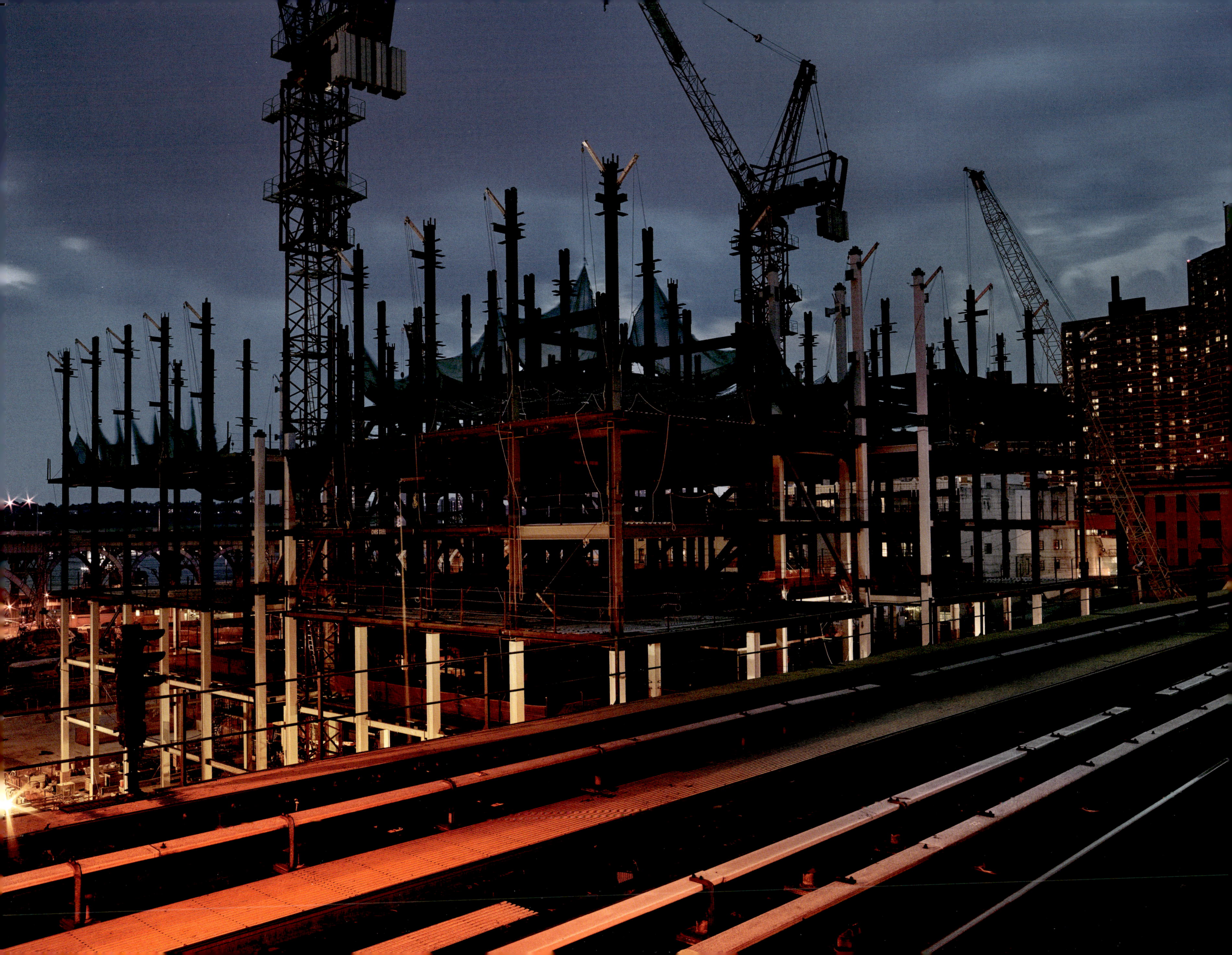

Boulevard, Santa Monica, California

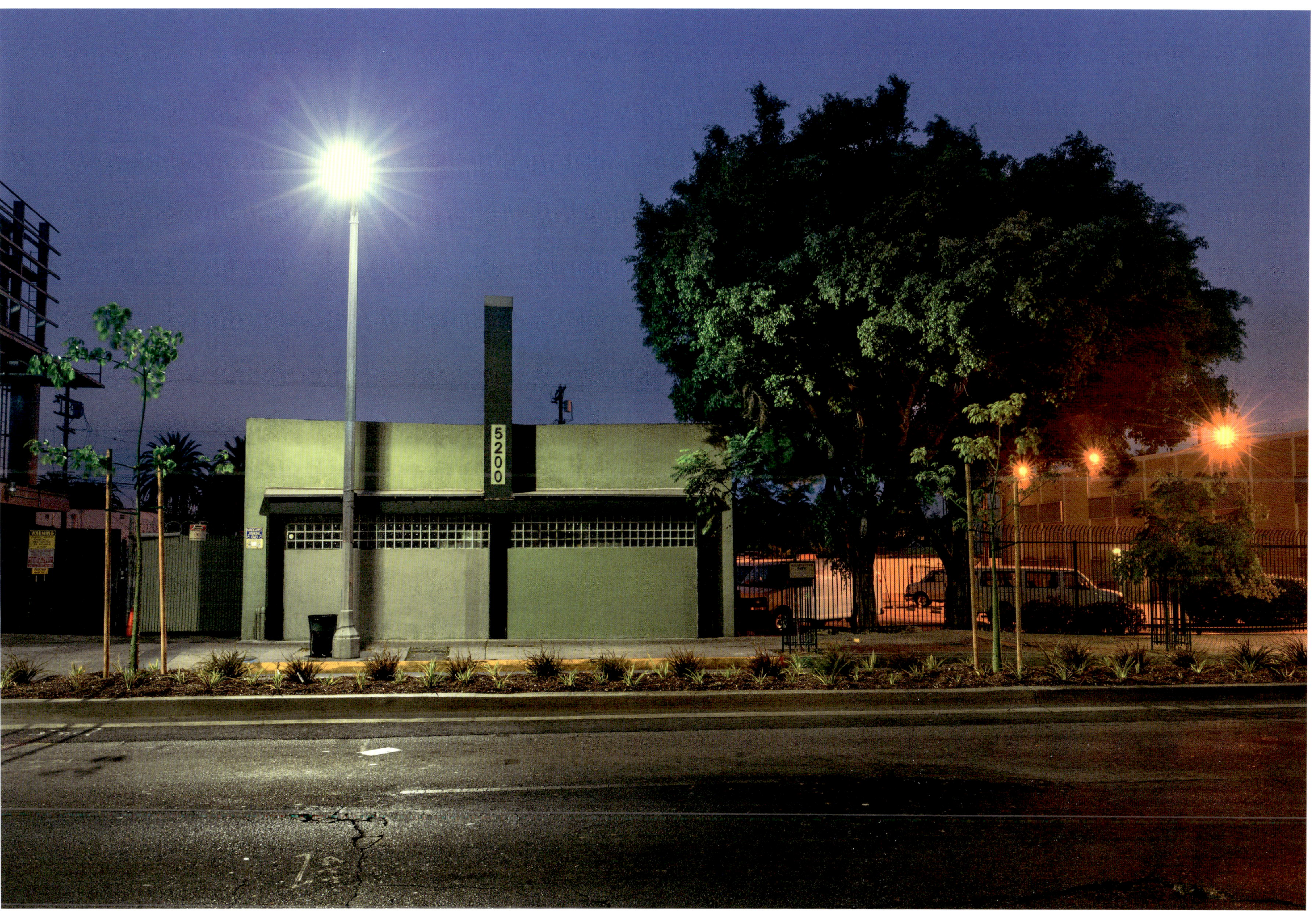
5200
WARNING

West 23rd Street, New York City

Page 42: Smith Street, Brooklyn, New York

Page 43: Cleveland City Banner, Cleveland, Ohio

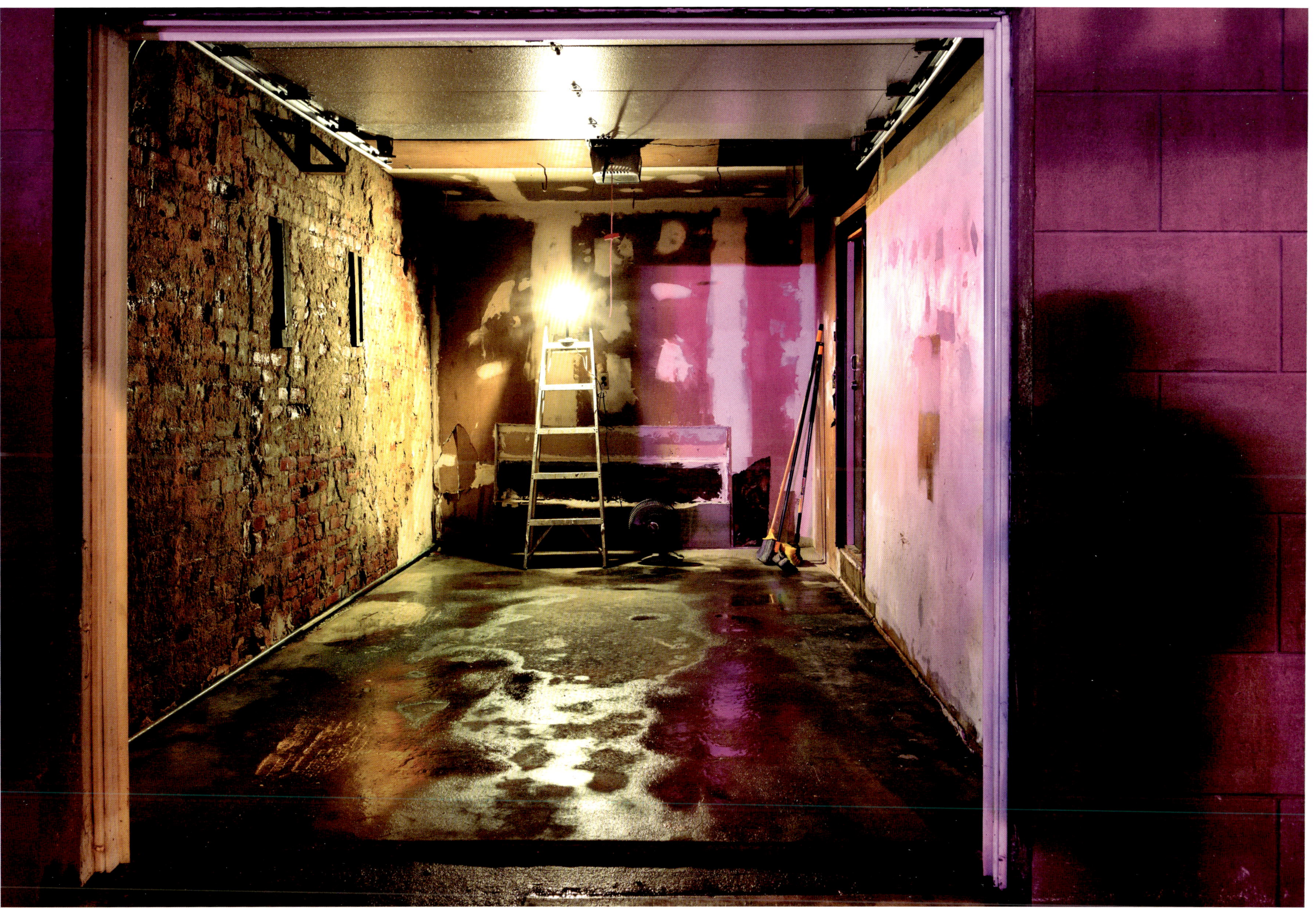

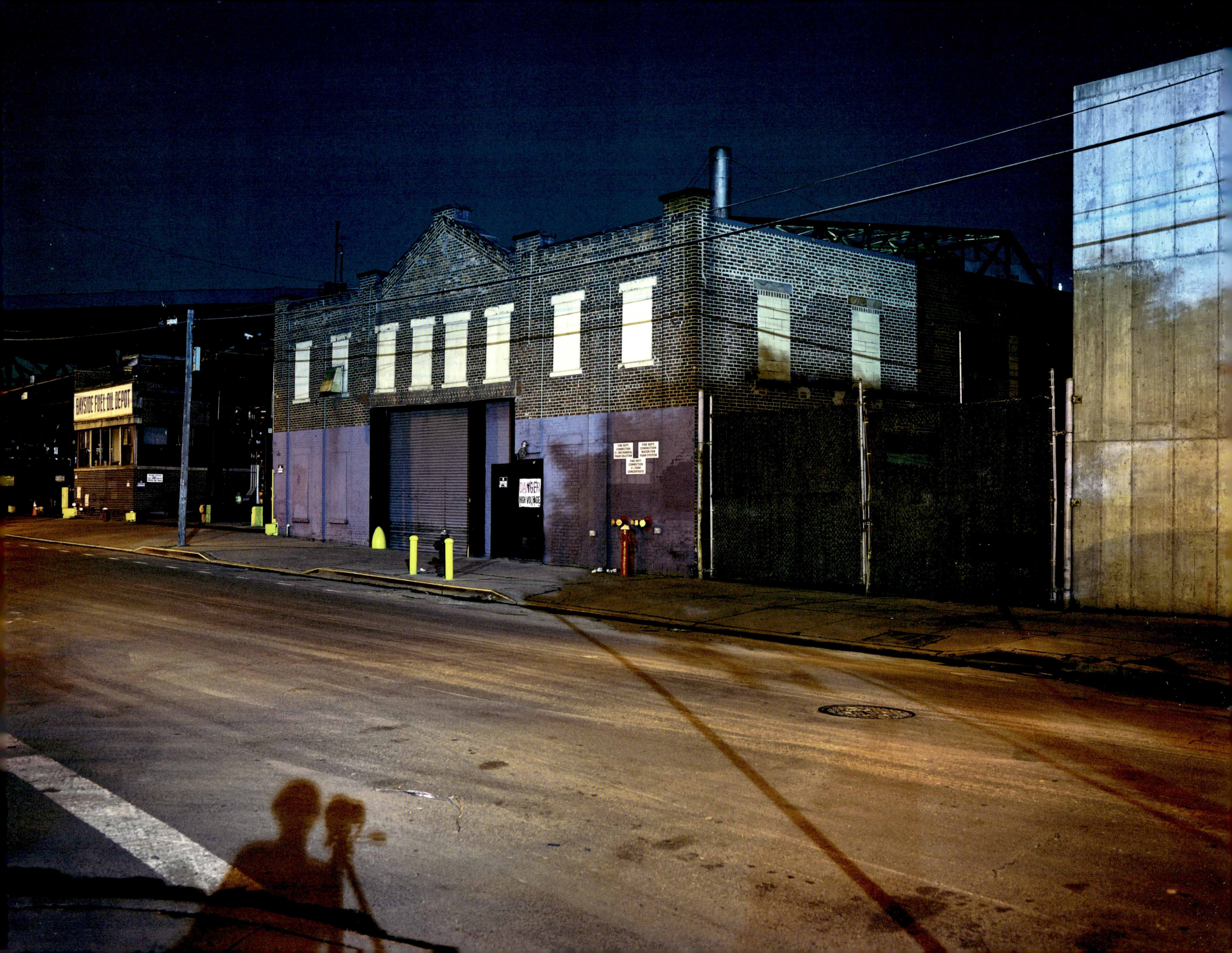
BAYSIDE FUEL OIL DEPOT
DANGER HIGH VOLTAGE
FIRE DEPT. CONNECTION 3% MECHANICAL FOAM SOLUTION
FIRE DEPT. CONNECTION WATER FOR FOAM SYSTEM
FIRE DEPT. CONNECTION 3% FORM CONCENTRATE

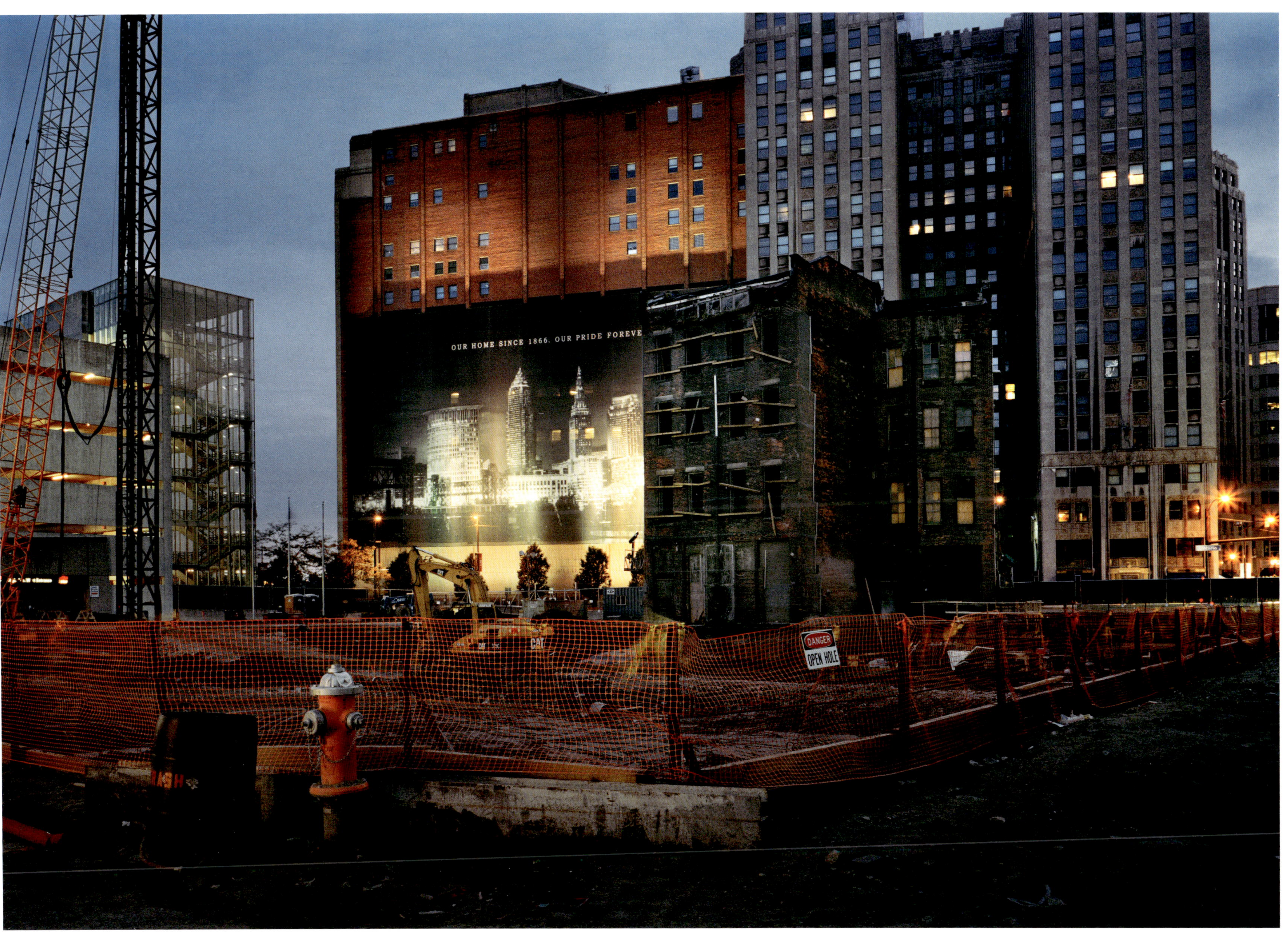
OUR HOME SINCE 1866. OUR PRIDE FOREVE
DANGER
OPEN HOLE
CAT

Warehouse, Greenpoint, Brooklyn, New York

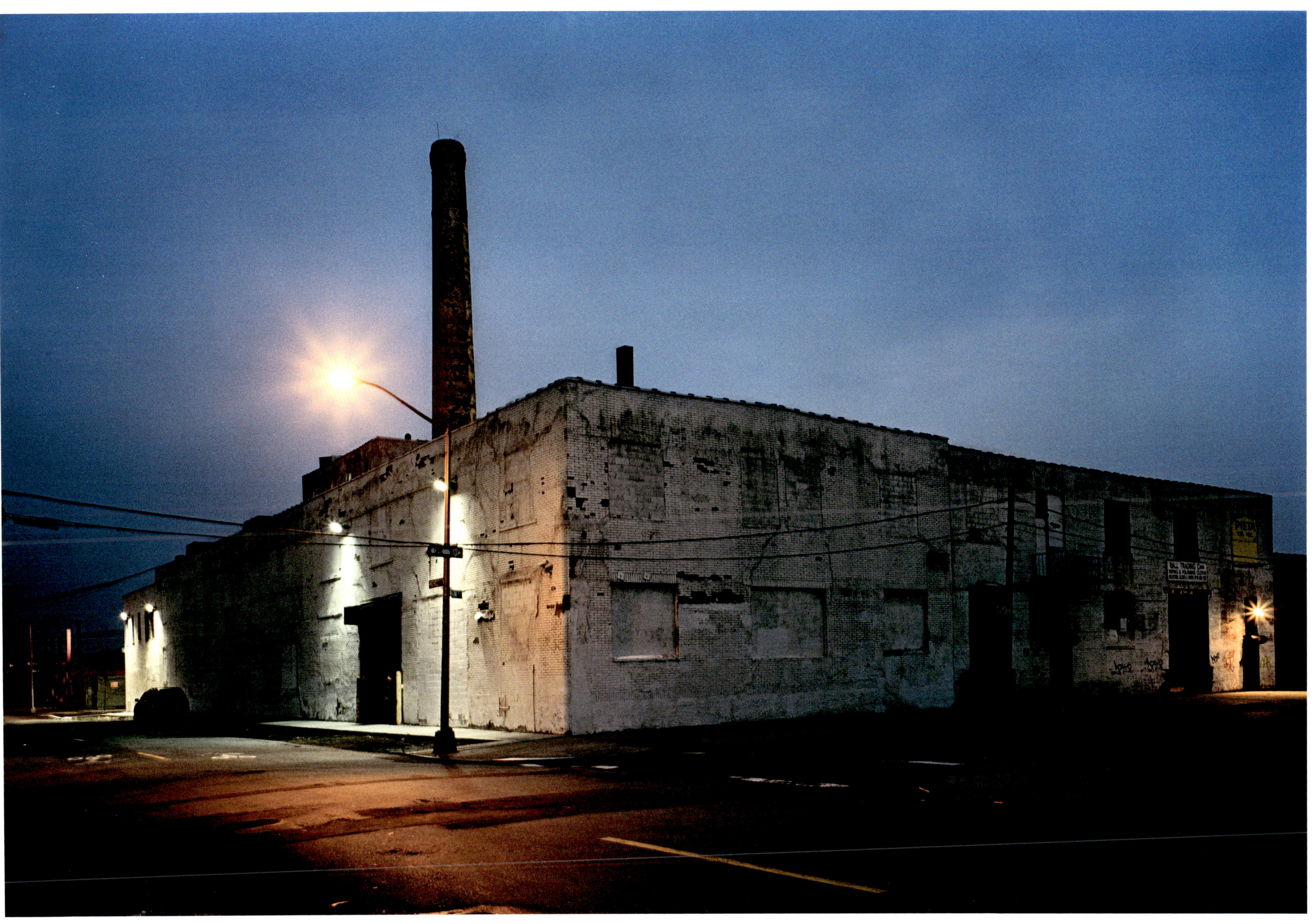

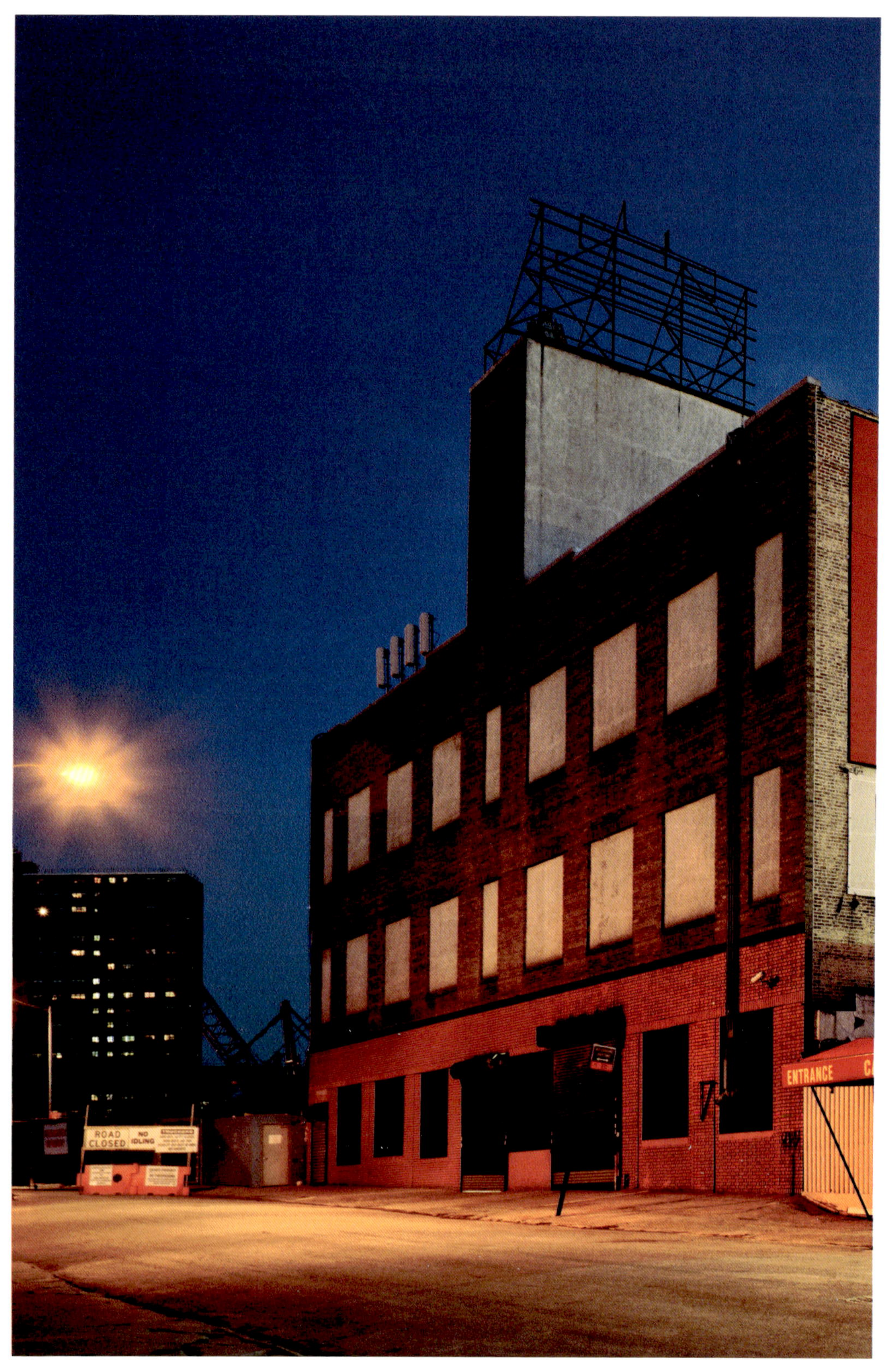

West Harlem, New York City

Opposite: Beneath the High Line, New York City

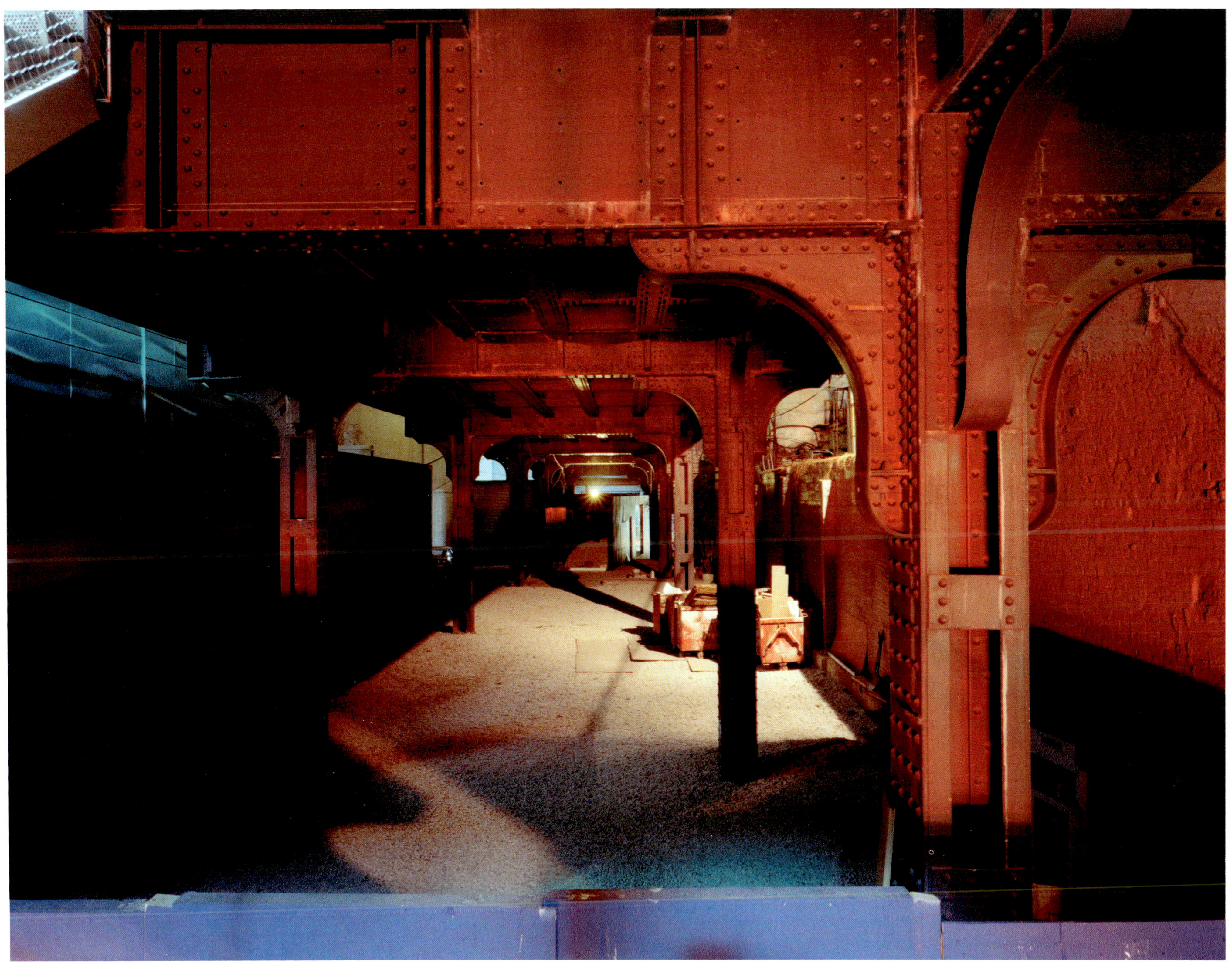

Hudson Street, New York City

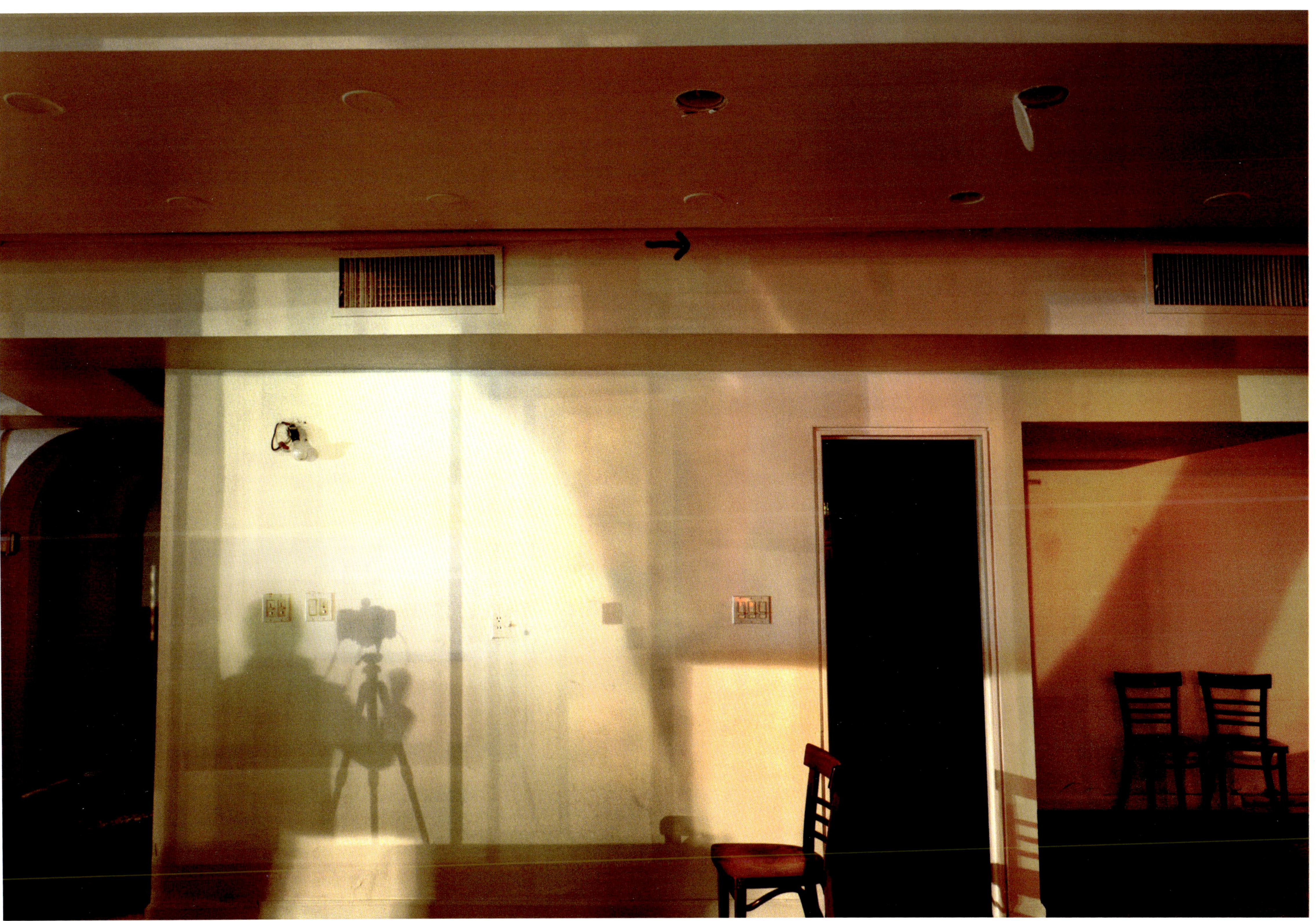

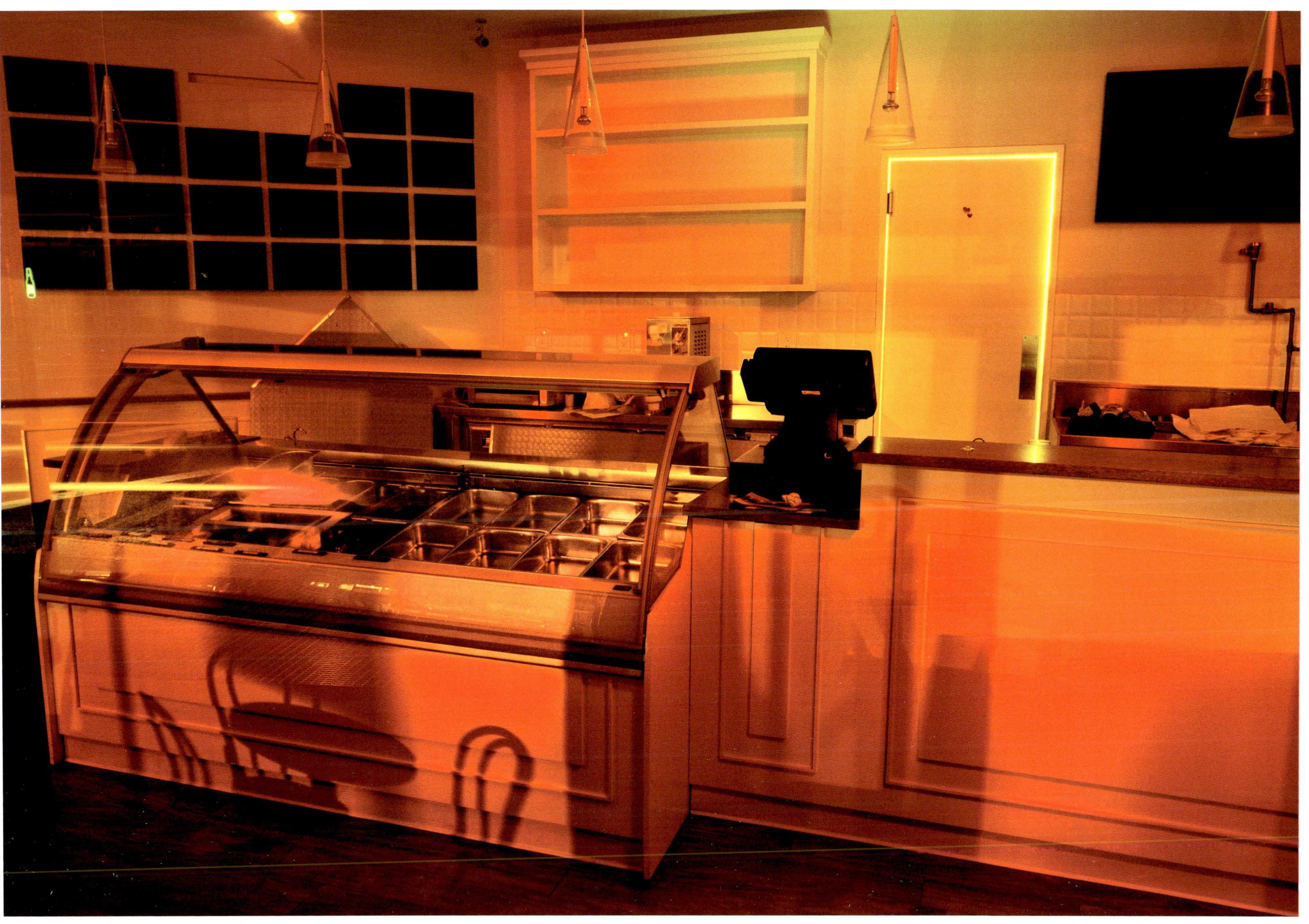

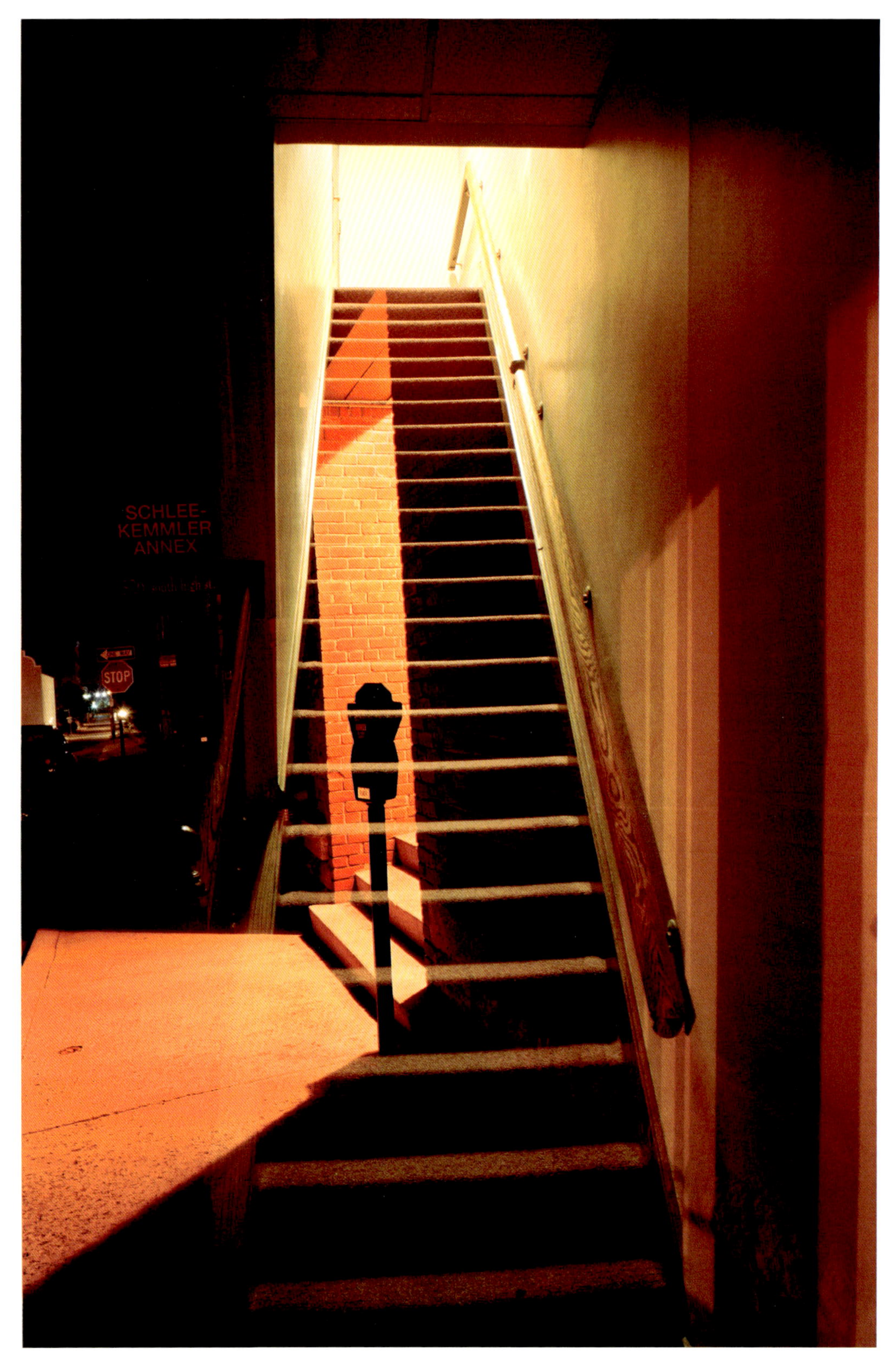

Stairway, Columbus, Ohio

Opposite: Lobby, Williamsburg,
Brooklyn, New York

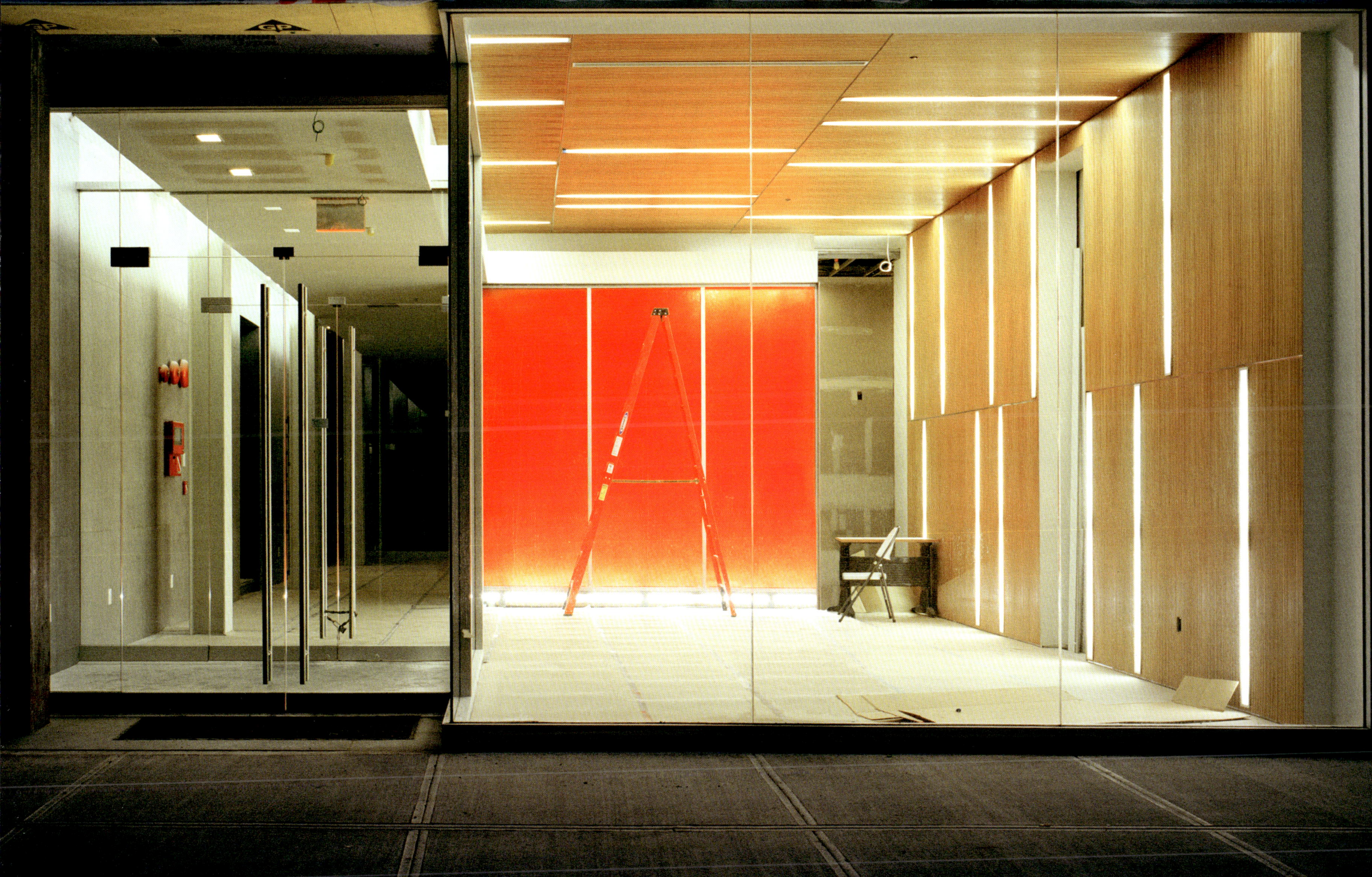

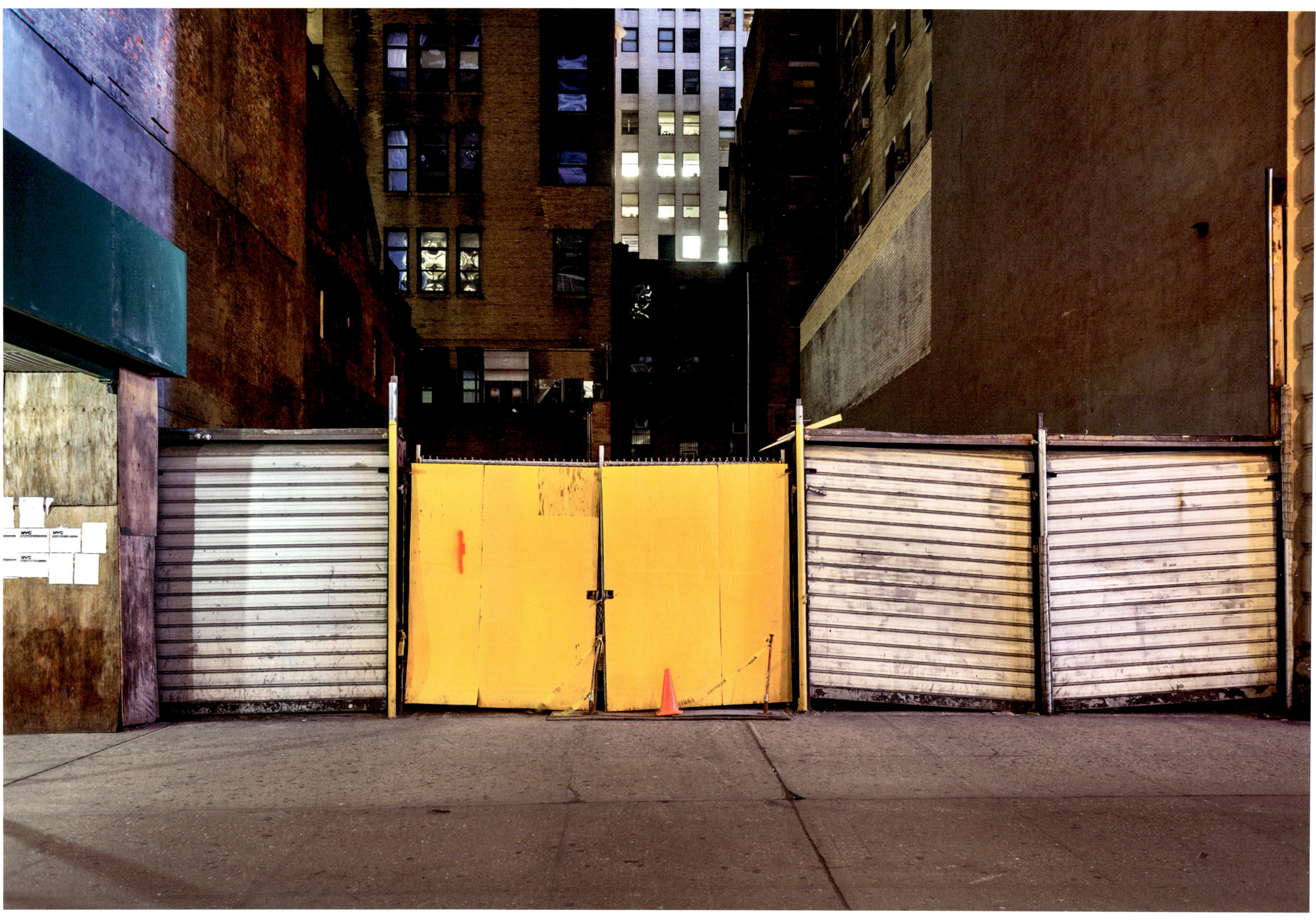

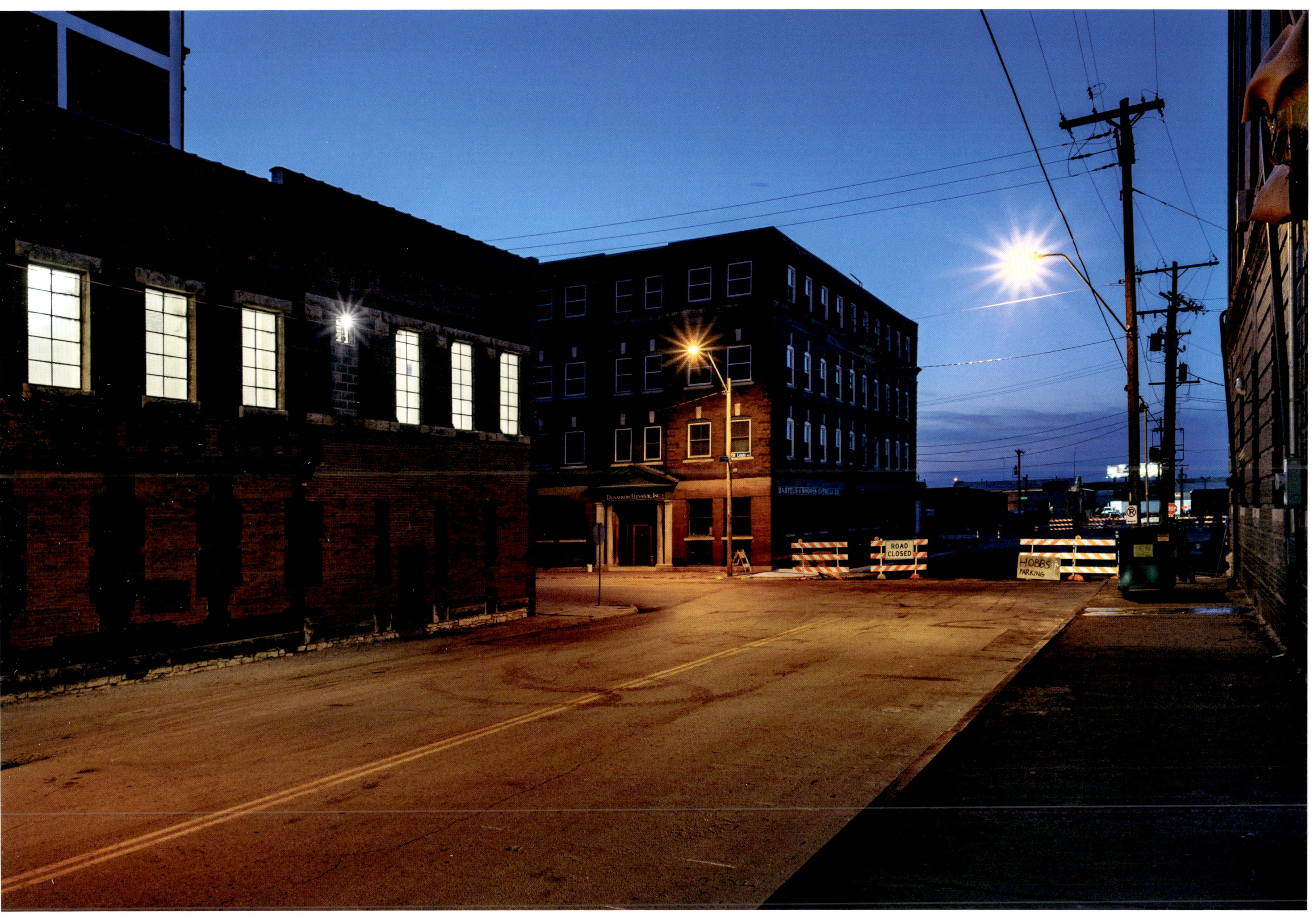

DYNATRON ELEVATOR, INC.
BARTELS & SHOREN CHEMICAL CO.
ROAD CLOSED
HOBBS PARKING

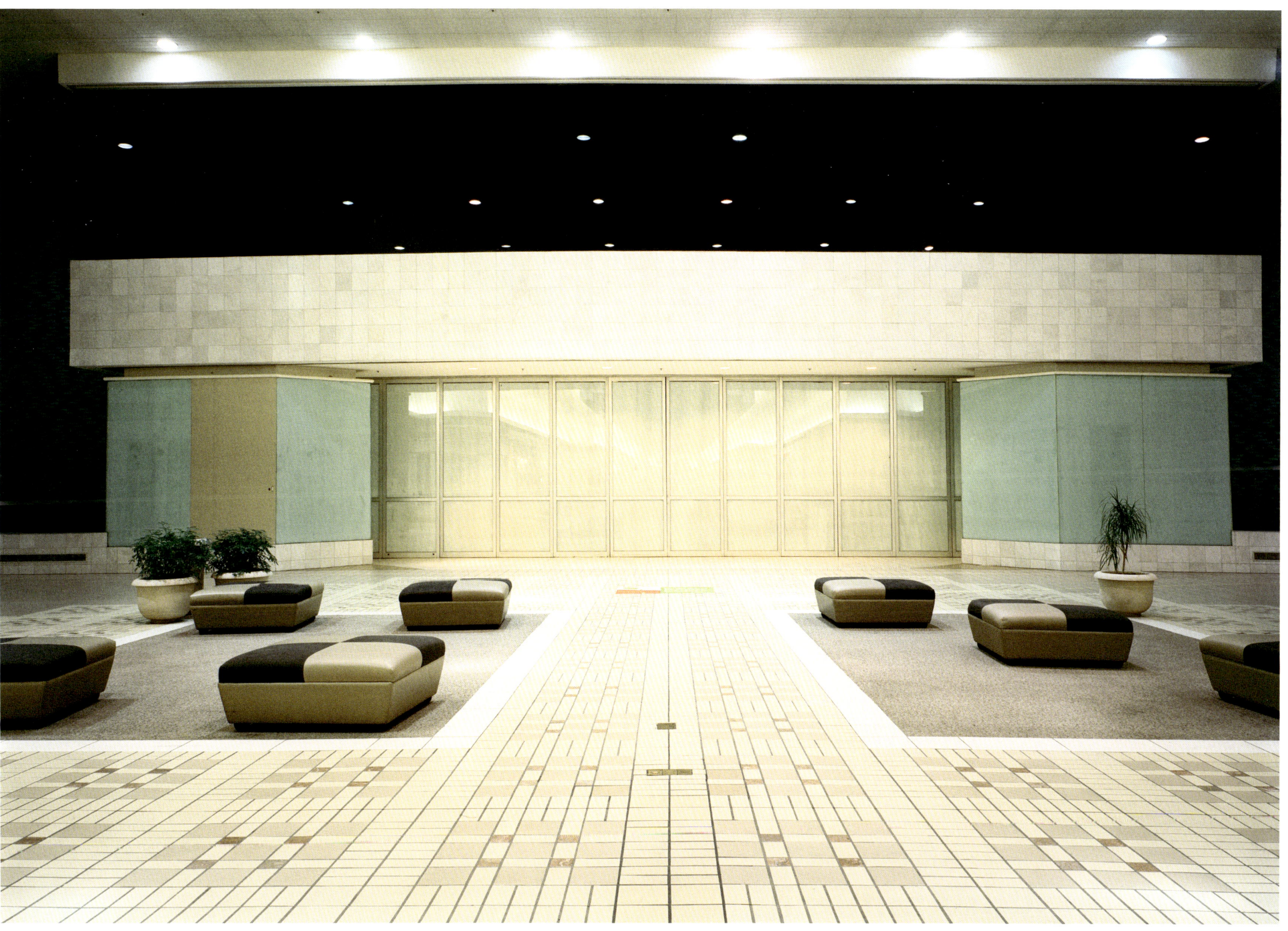

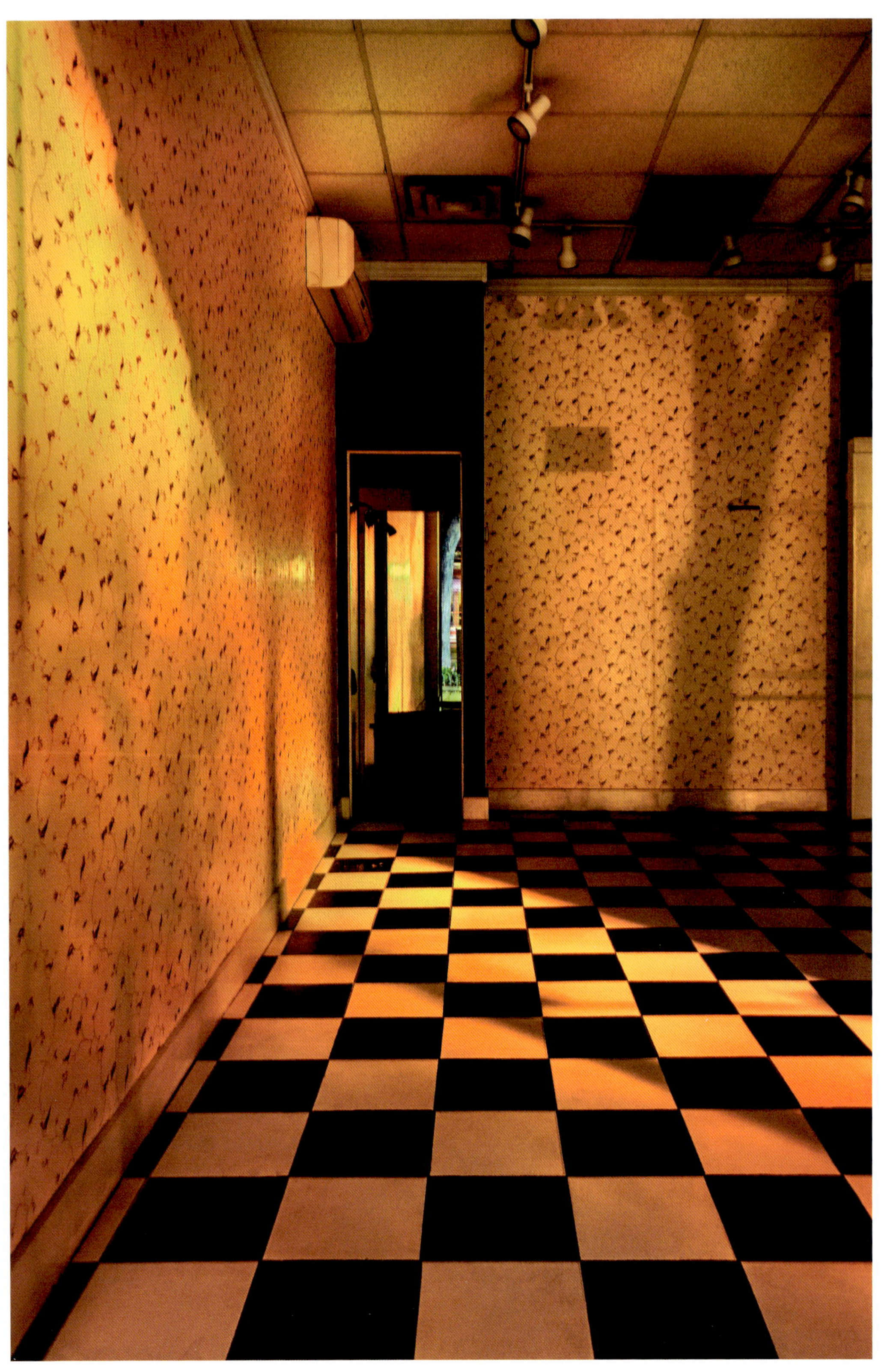

Former Boutique, Amsterdam Avenue, New York City

Opposite: Fishtown, Philadelphia, Pennsylvania

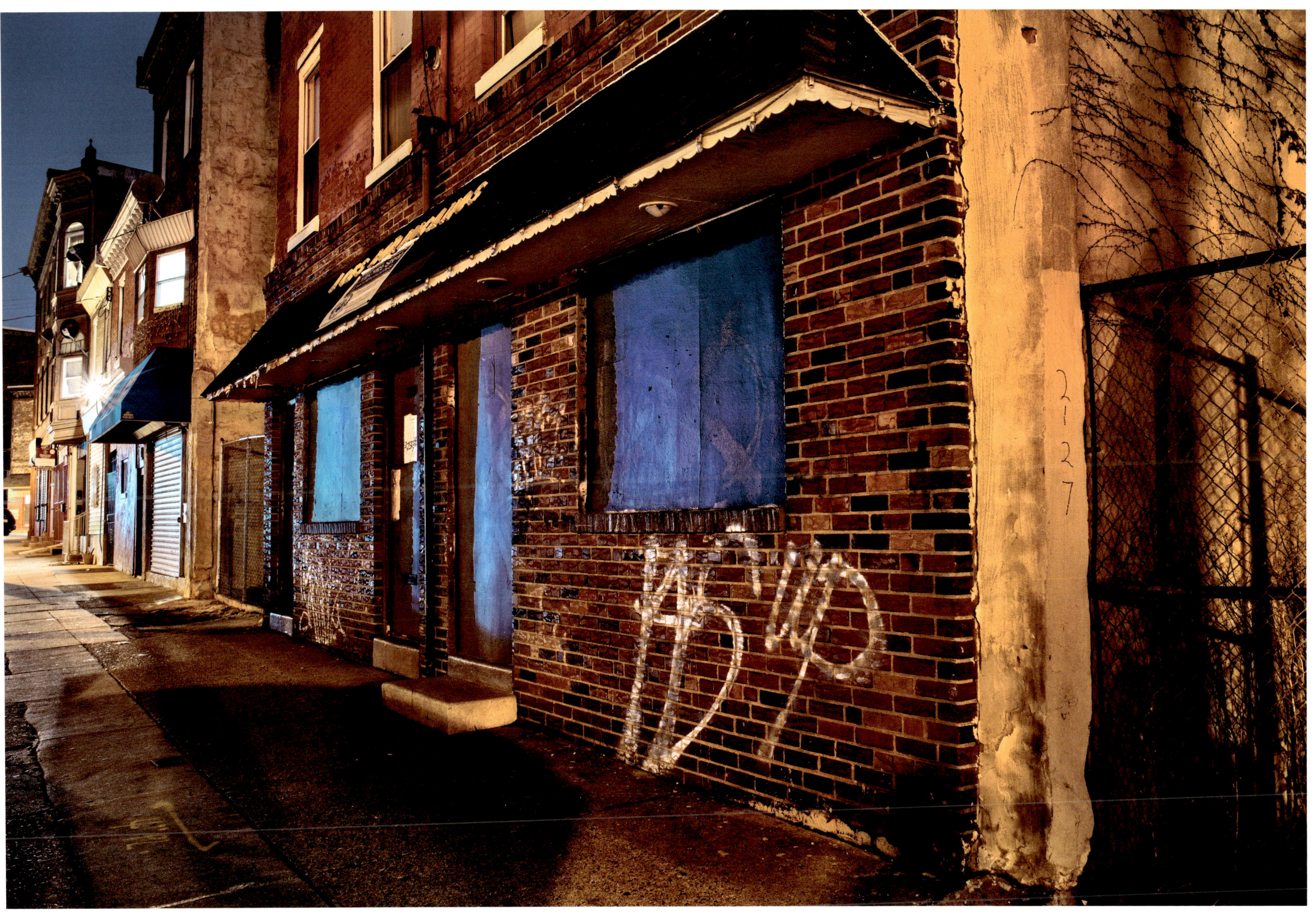

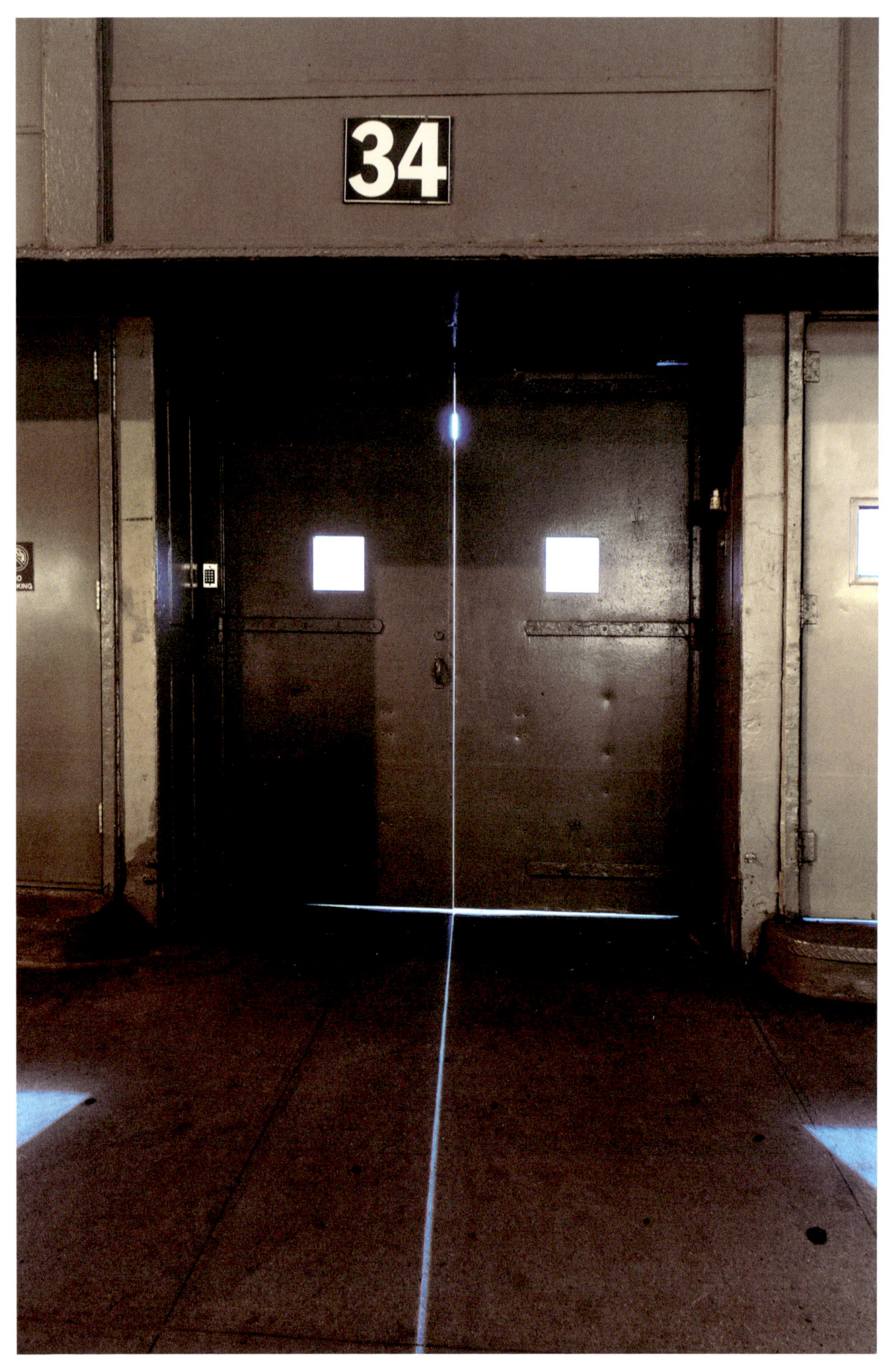

West 26th Street, New York City

Opposite: Former Gas Station, Washington, D.C.

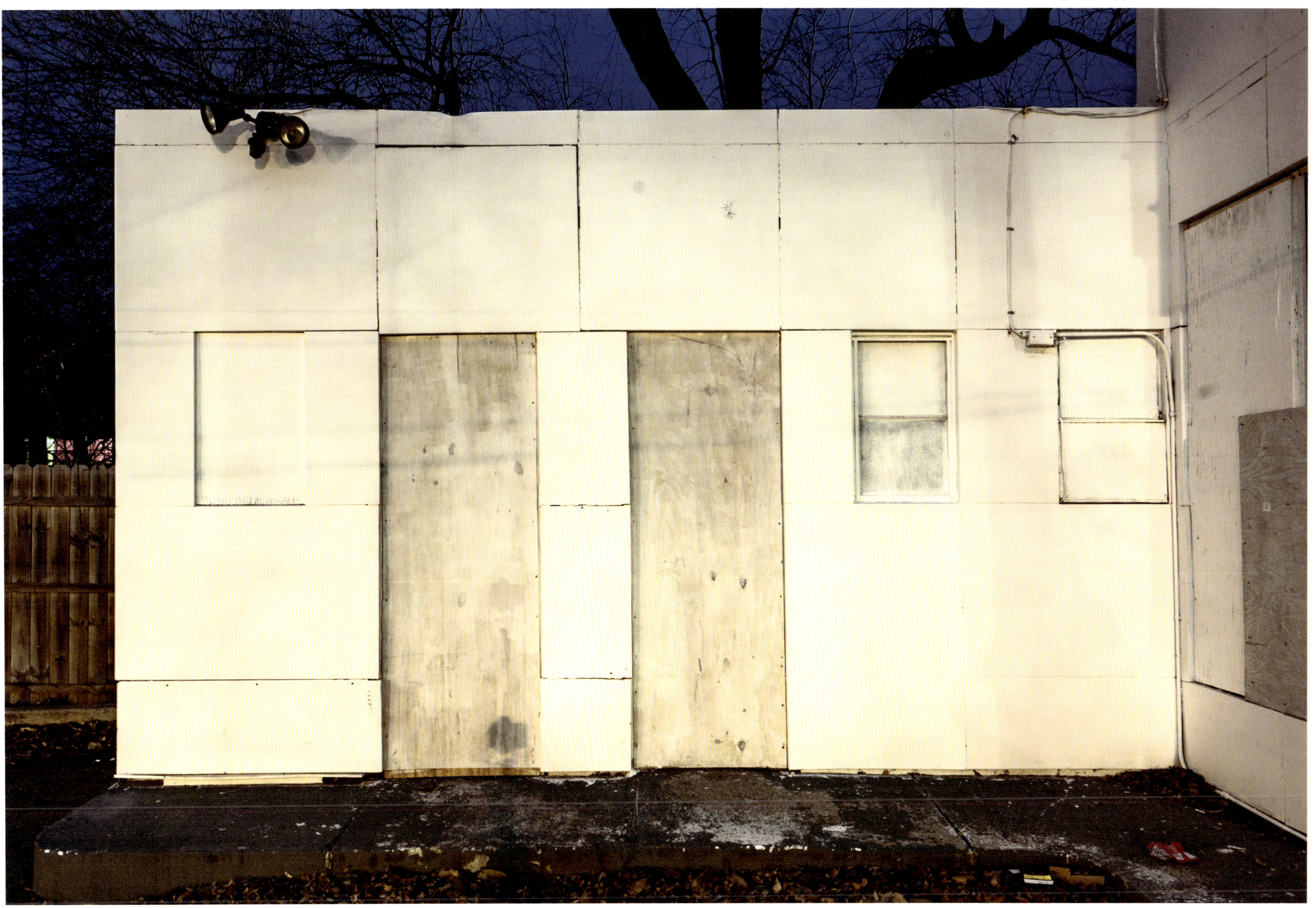

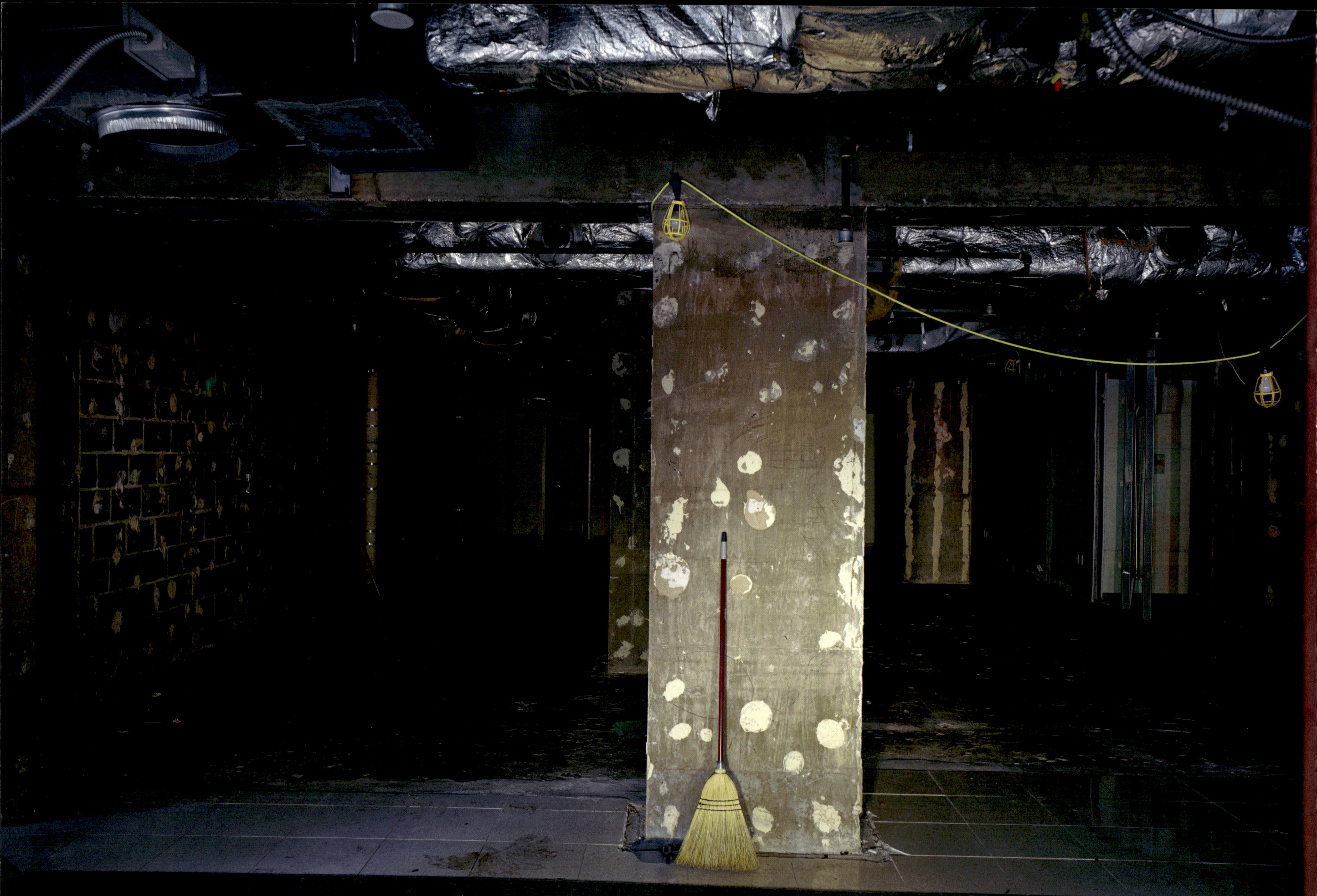

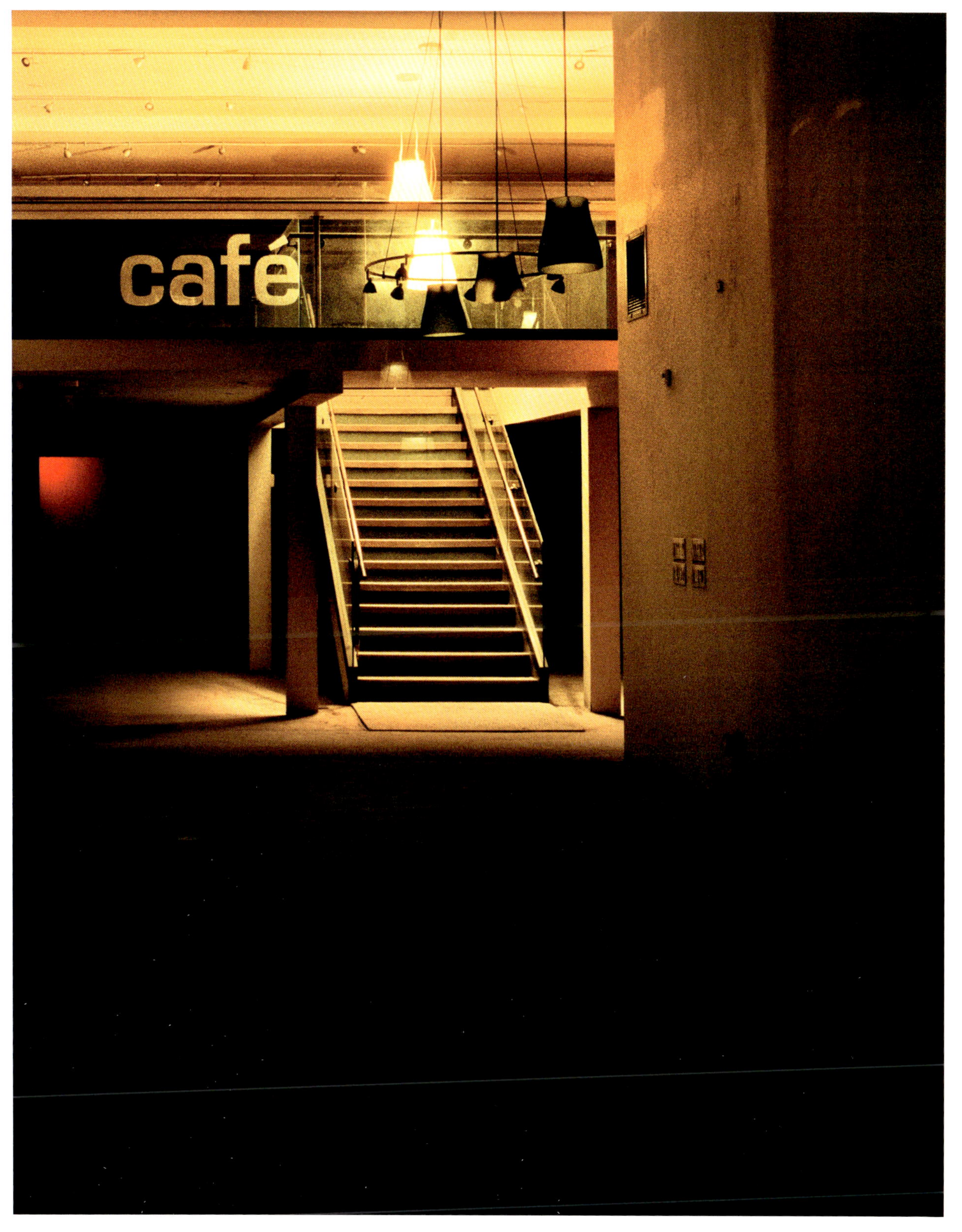

Opposite: Amsterdam Avenue, New York City

Former East West Bookshop, Fifth Avenue,
New York City

Former Gas Station, Chelsea, New York City

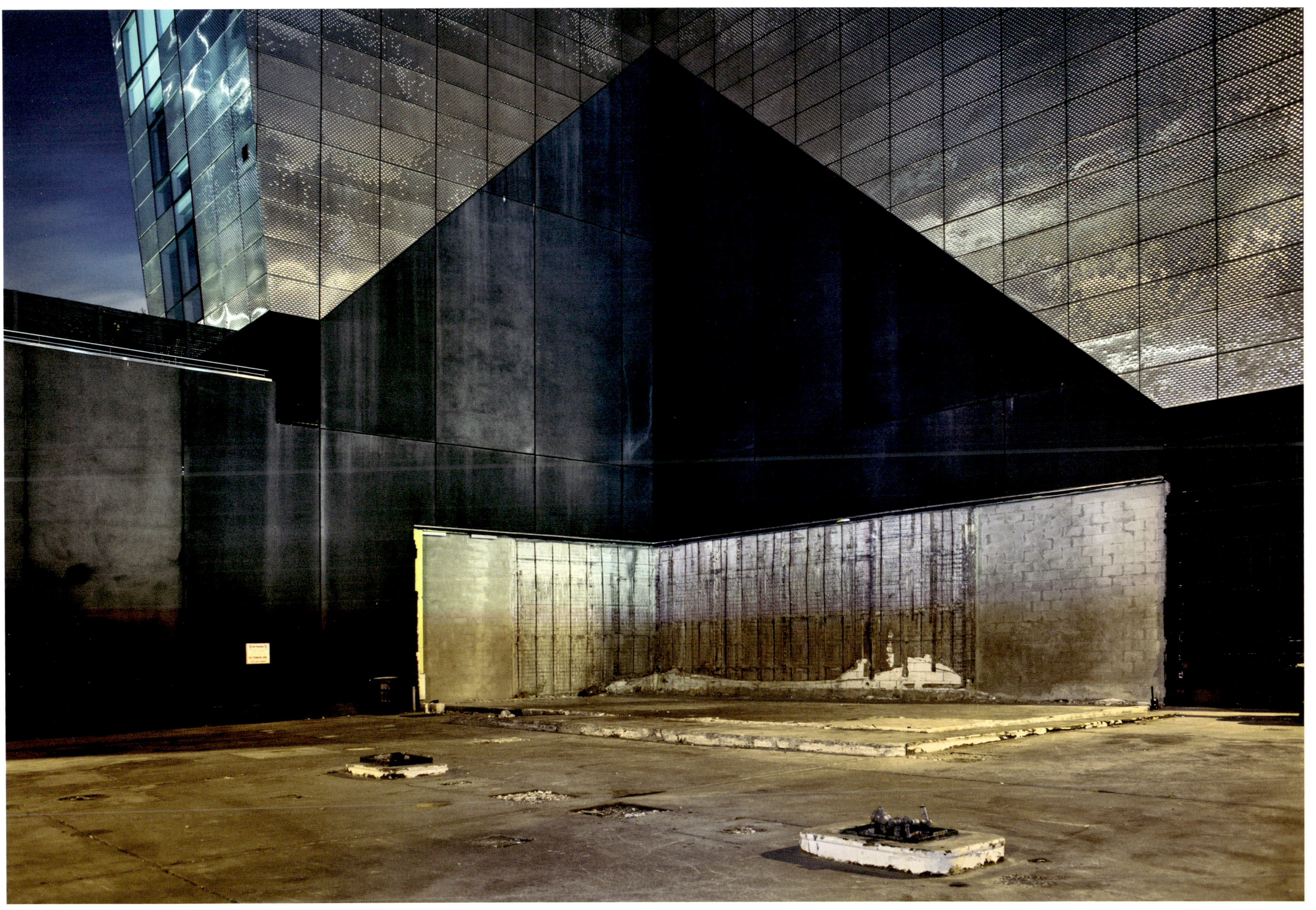

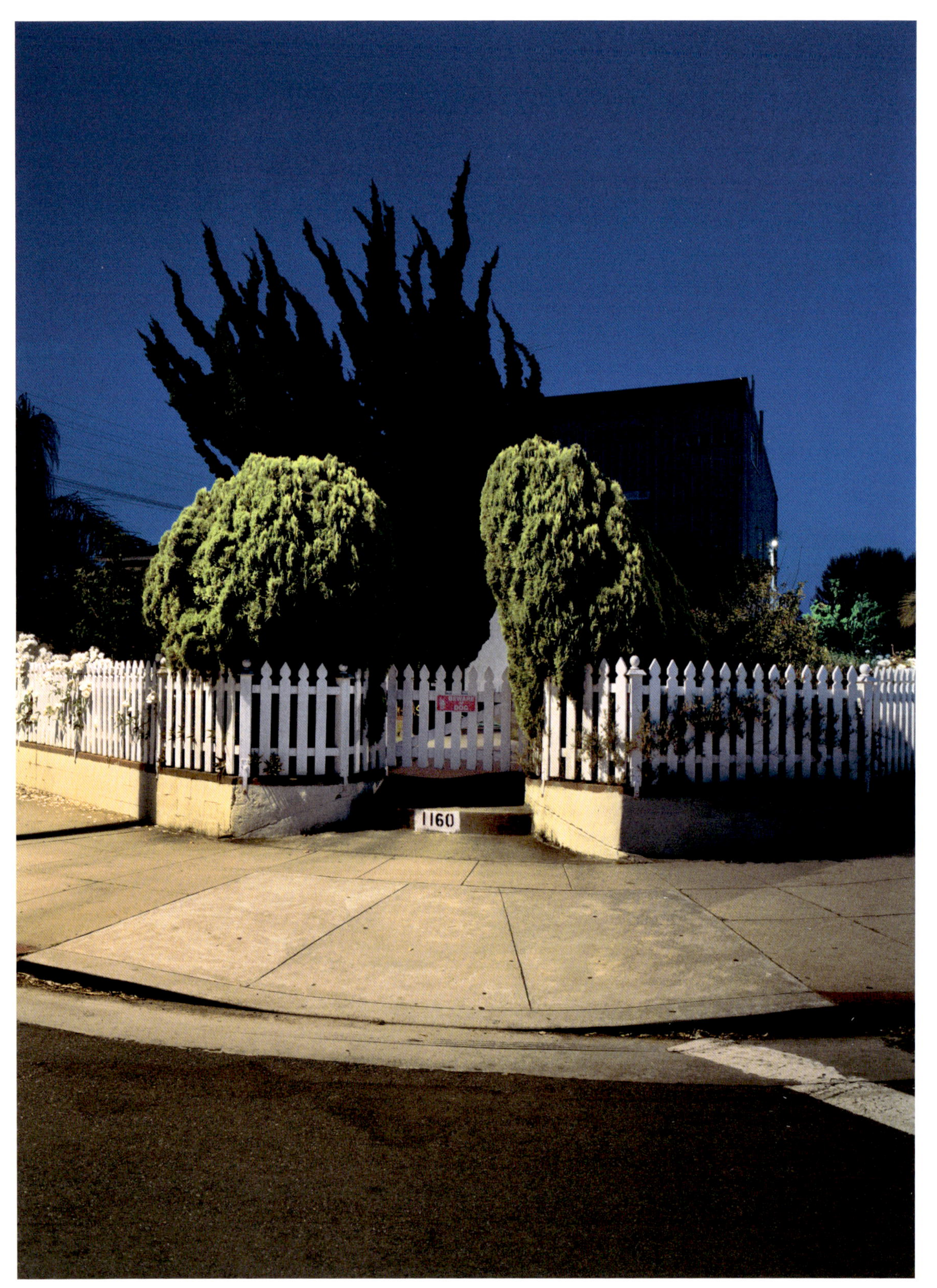

Penmar Avenue, Venice, California

Opposite: Corner Storefront,
Santa Monica, California

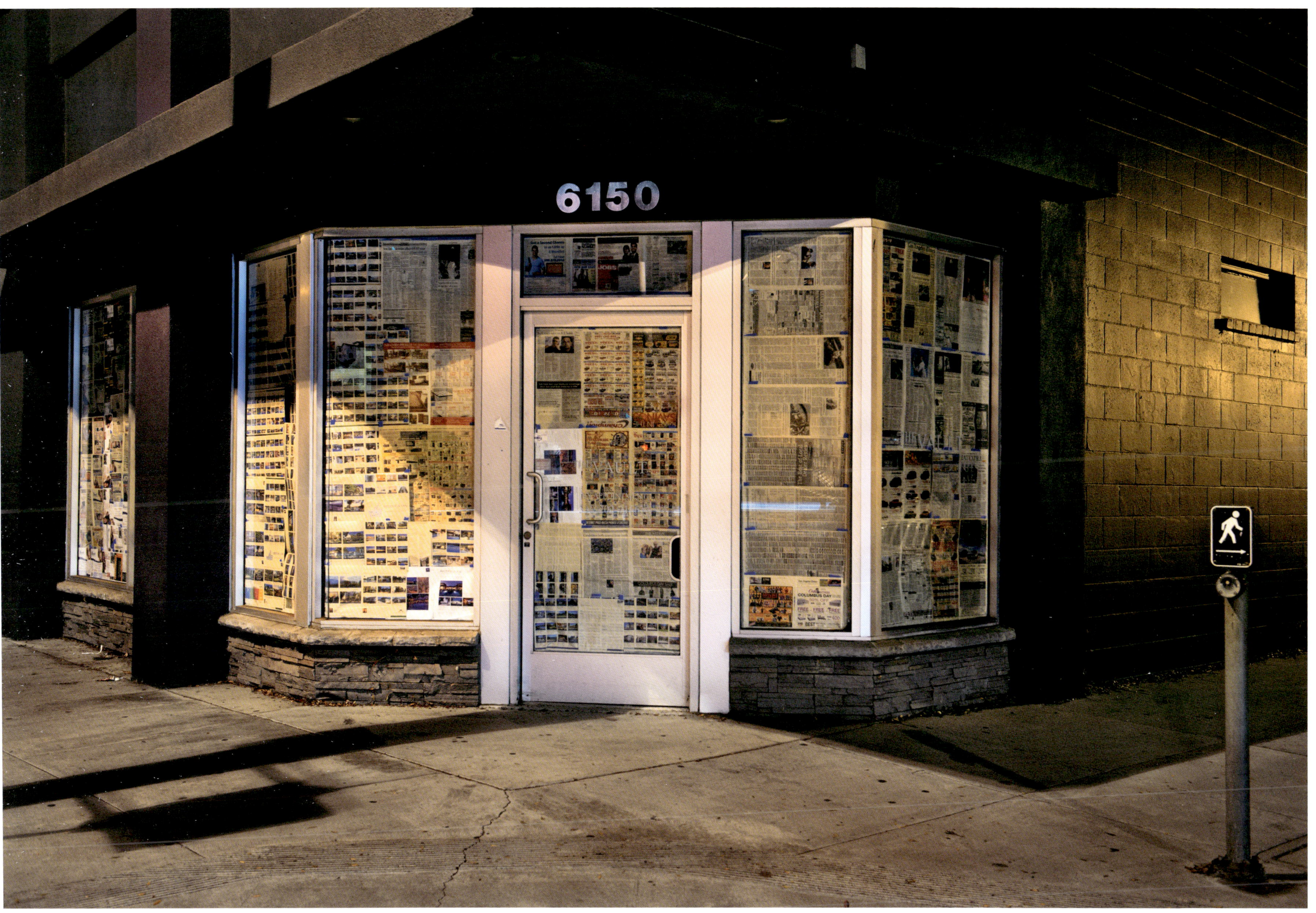

6150

La Floridita, Broadway, New York City

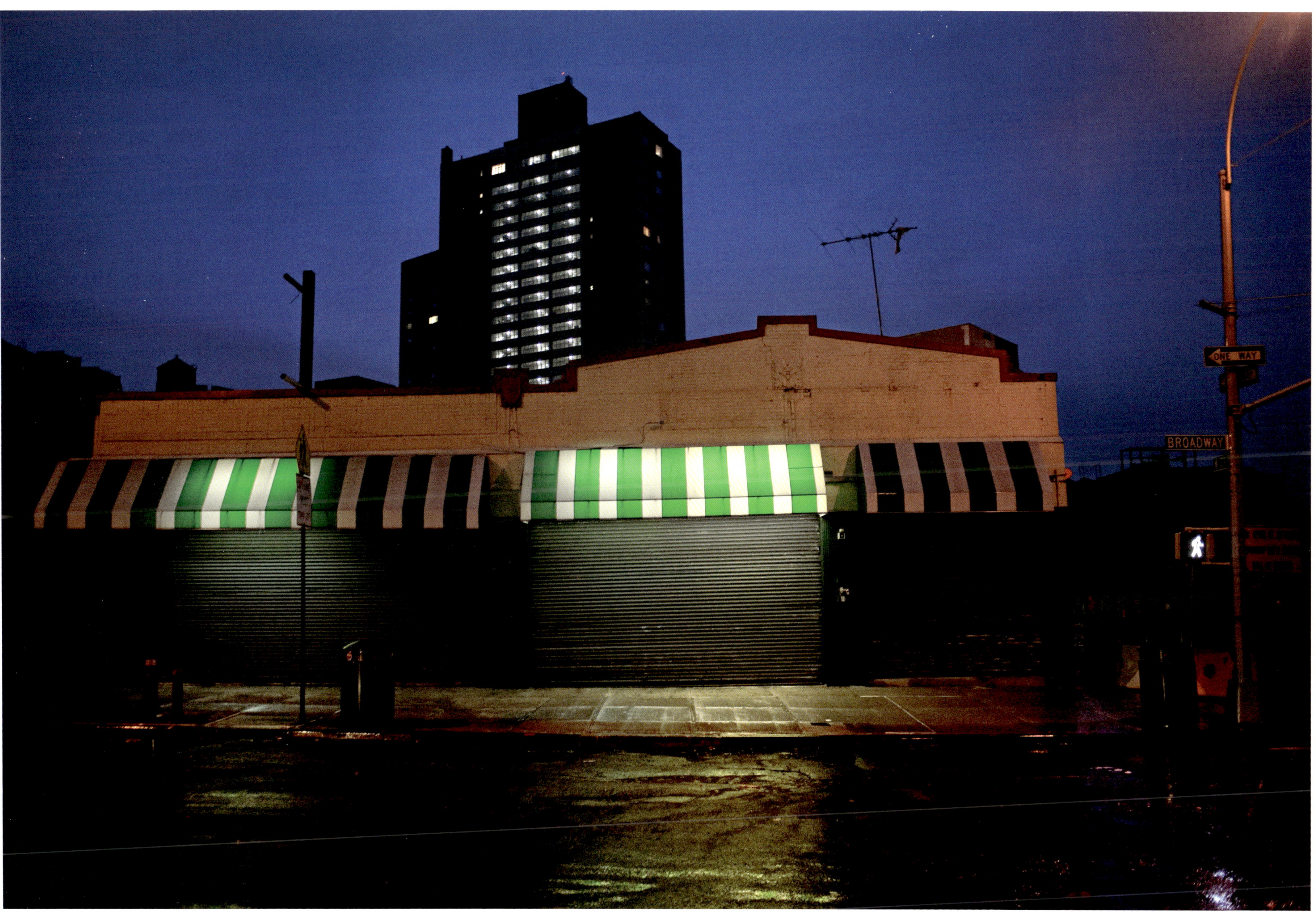

ONE WAY
BROADWAY

Burlington, Vermont

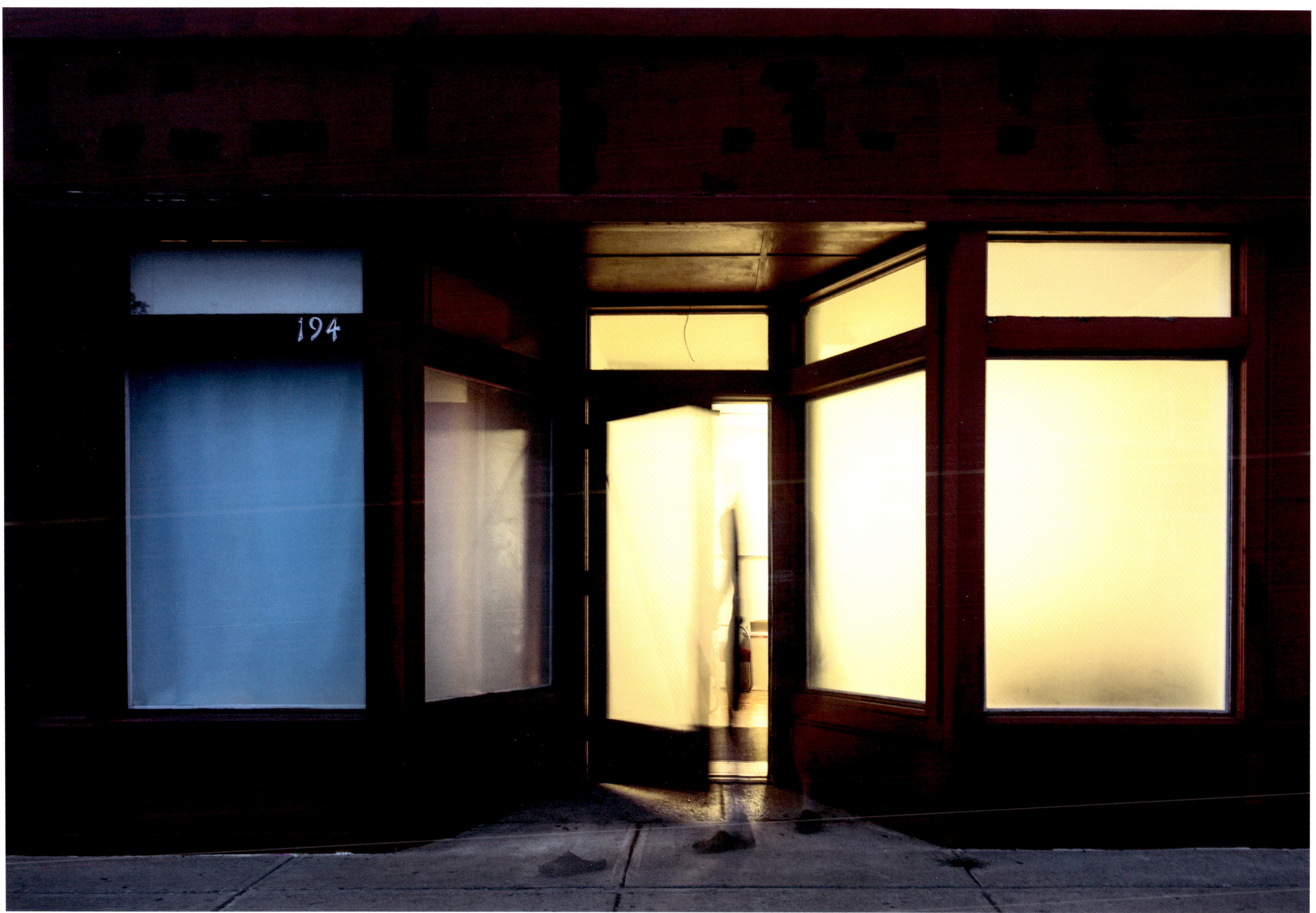

194

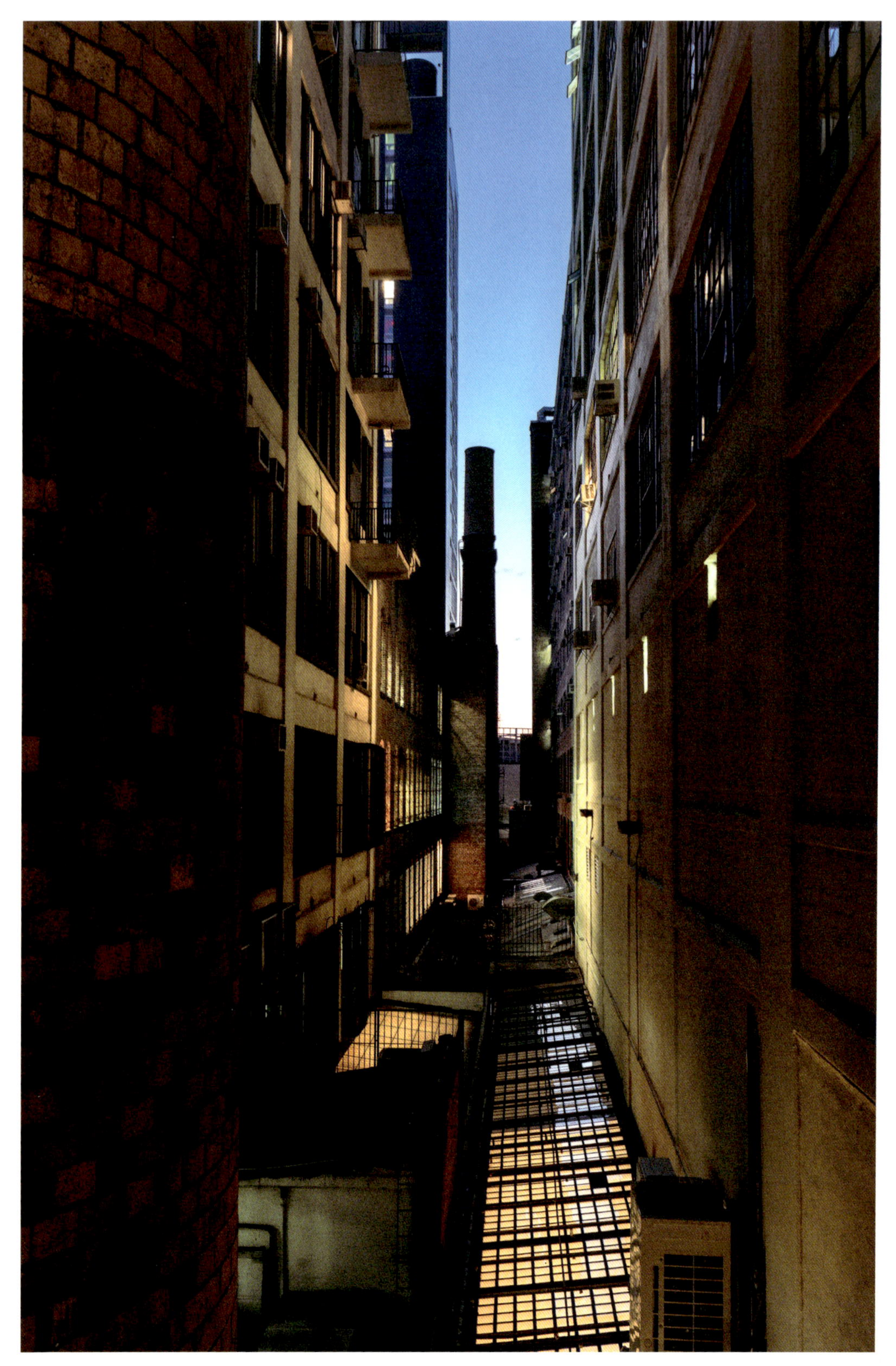

Alley from High Line, New York City

Opposite: Front Street, Brooklyn, New York

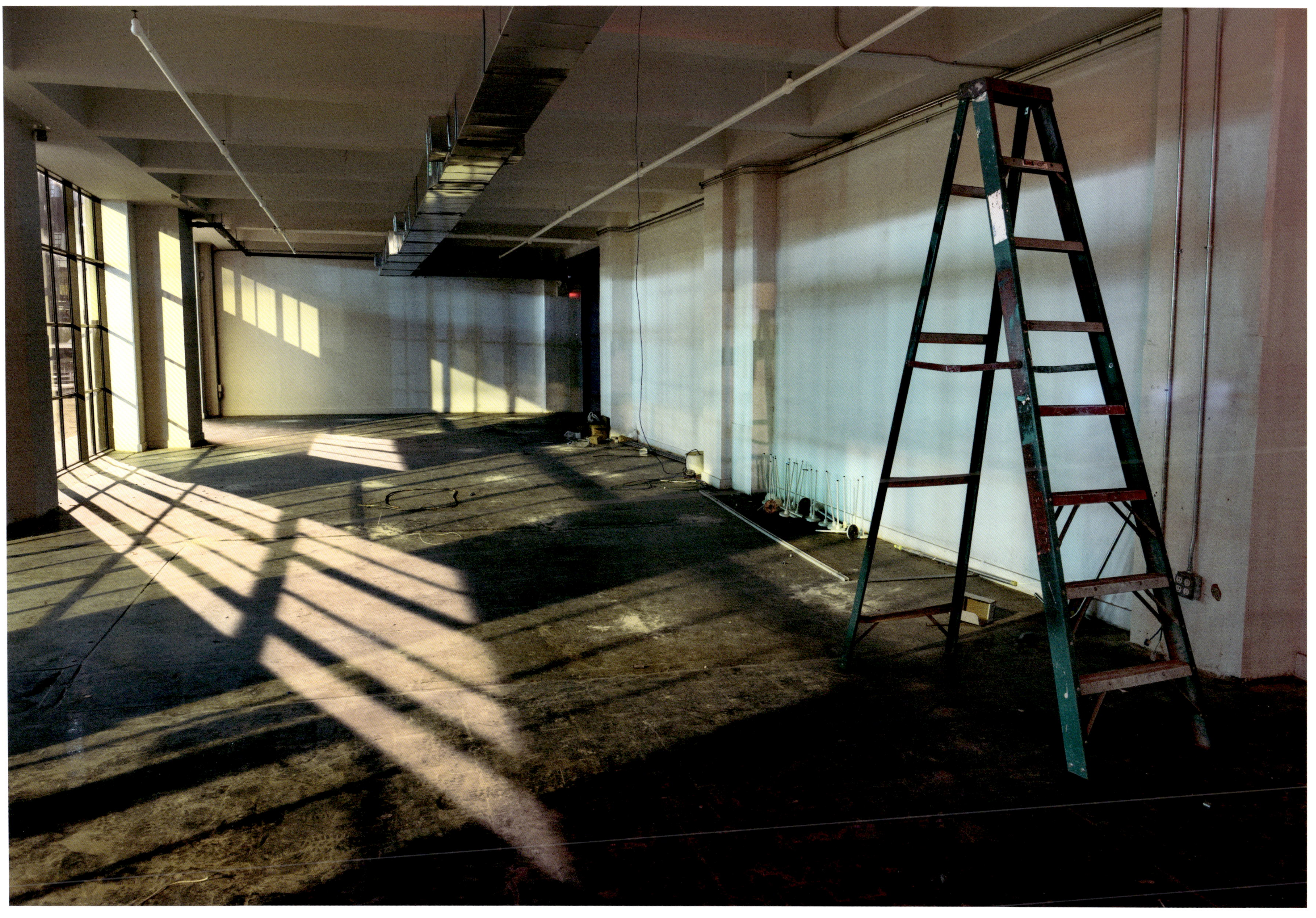

Restaurant Under Construction, Troy, New York

Page 76: Construction Site, Chelsea, New York City

Page 77: Mural, 9th Avenue at 42nd Street, New York City

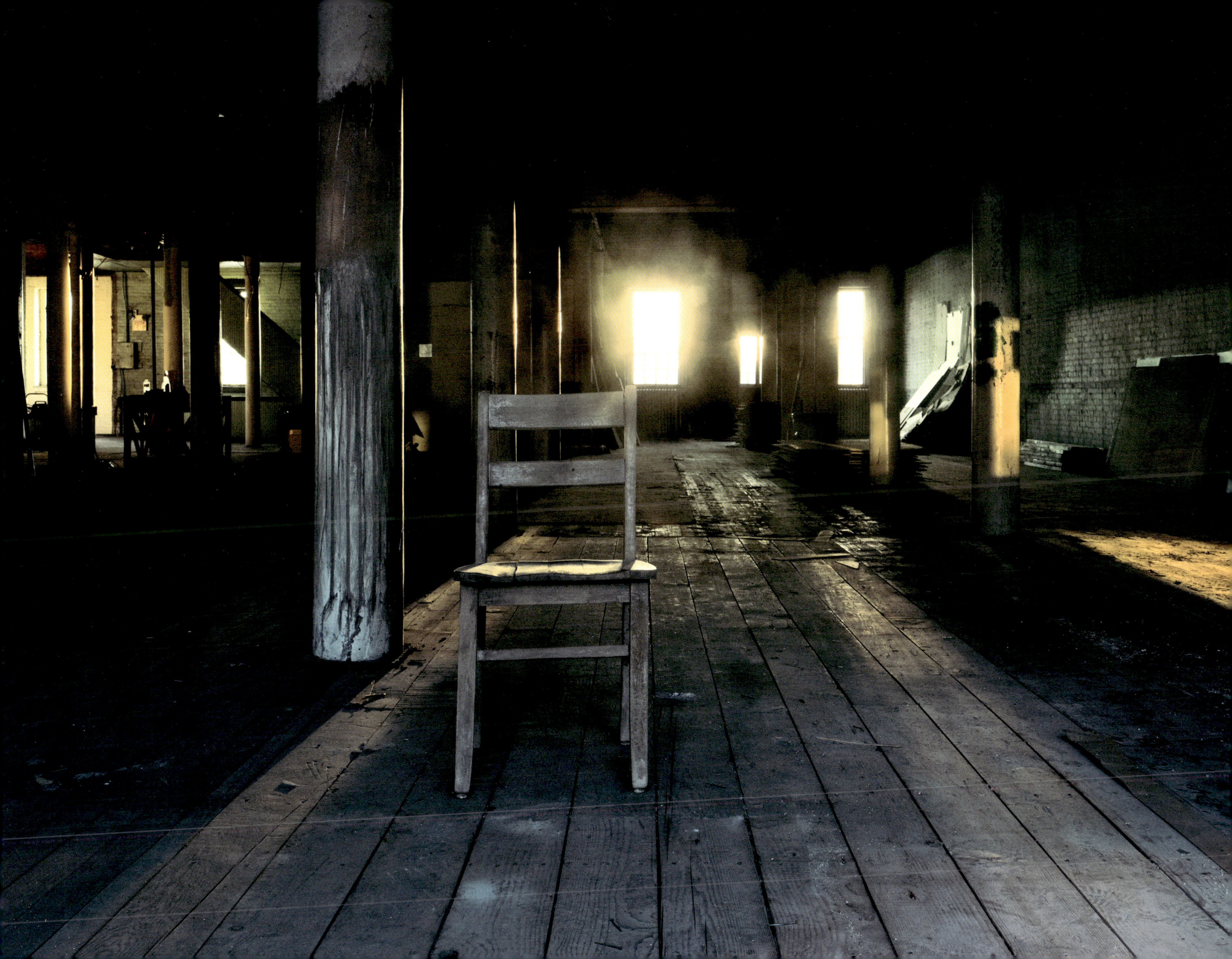

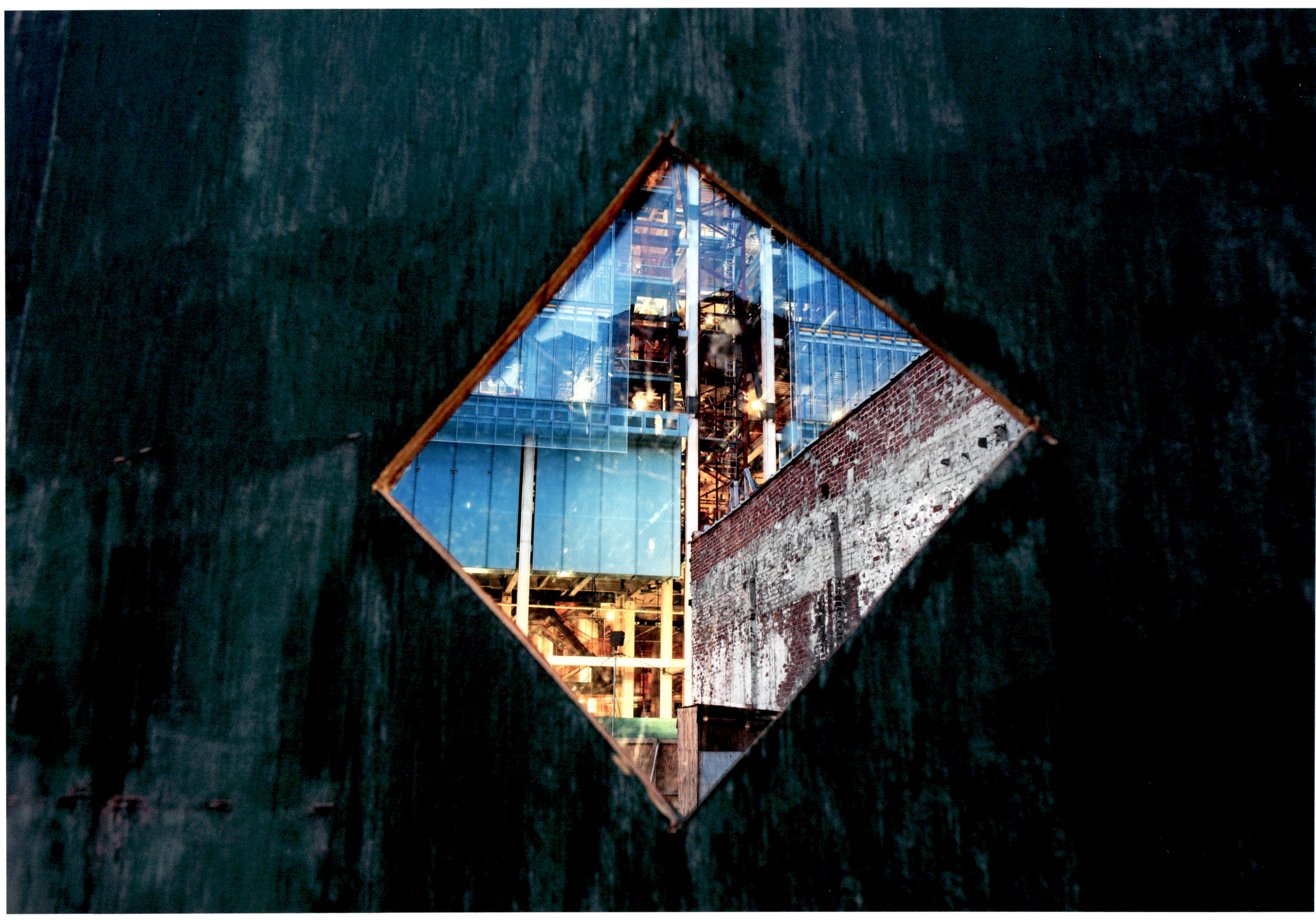

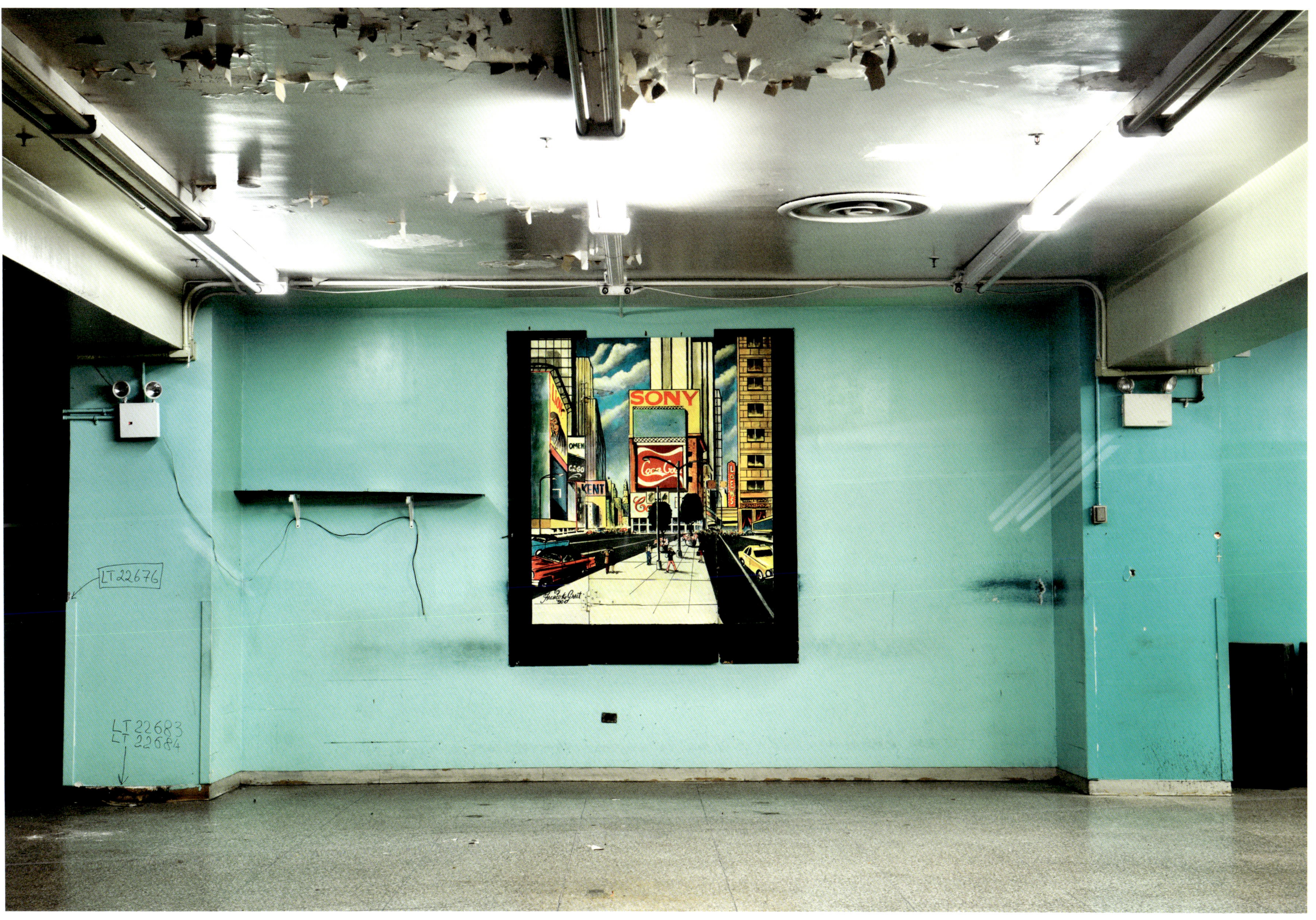
LT 22676
LT 22683
LT 22684
SONY
Coca-Cola
KENT
LOEWS

West 126th Street, New York City

Pages 80–81: Warehouses, Houston, Texas

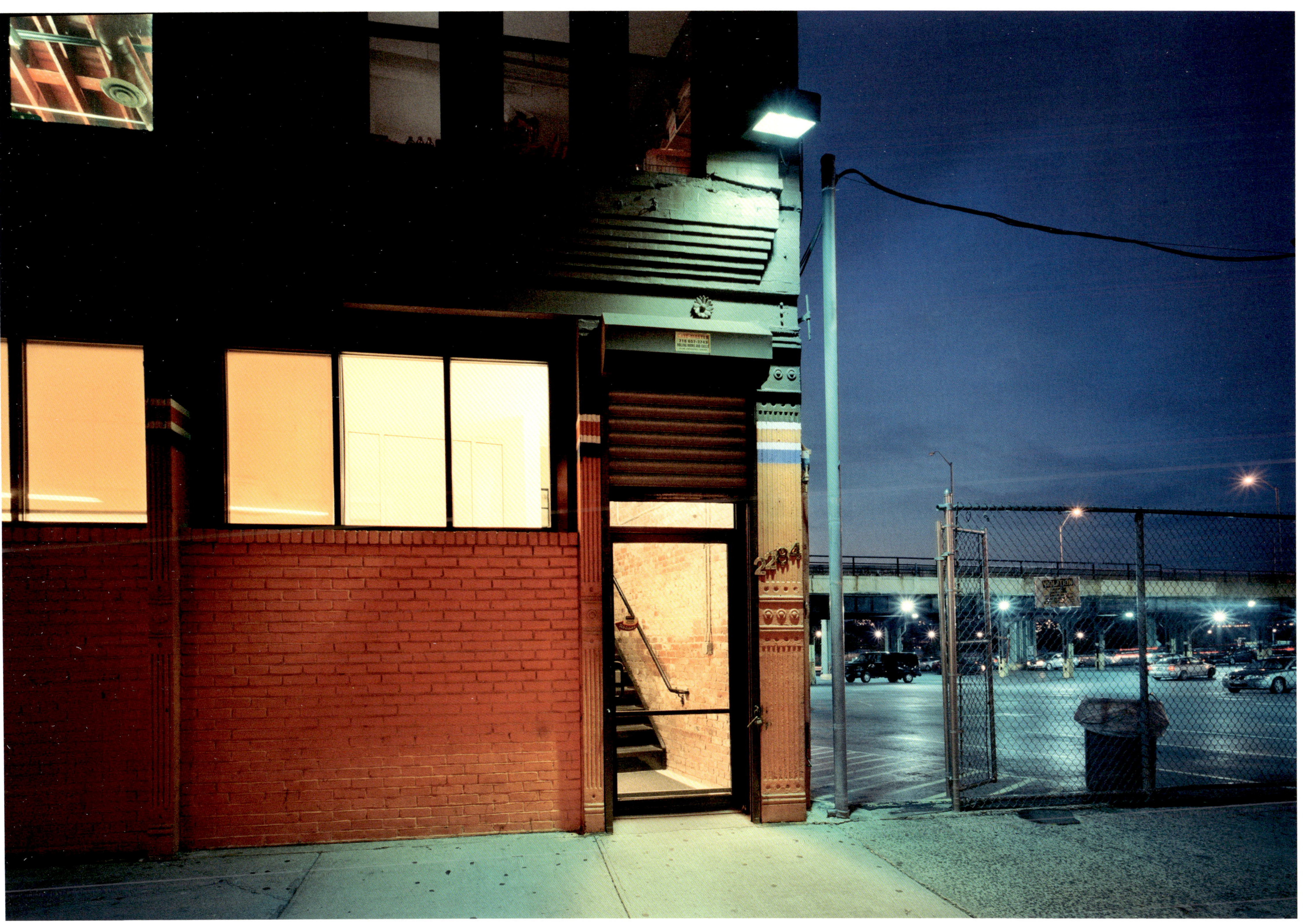

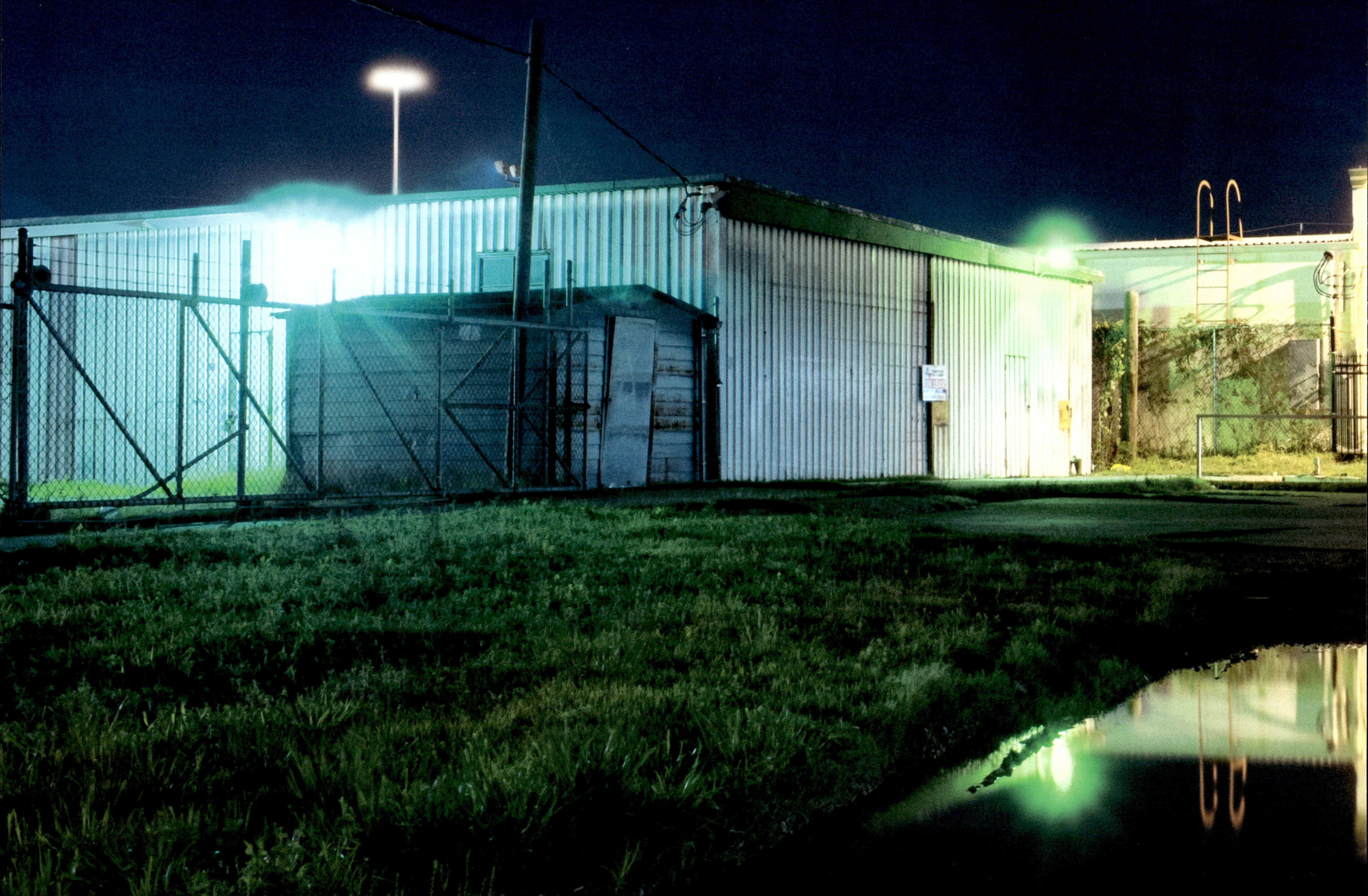

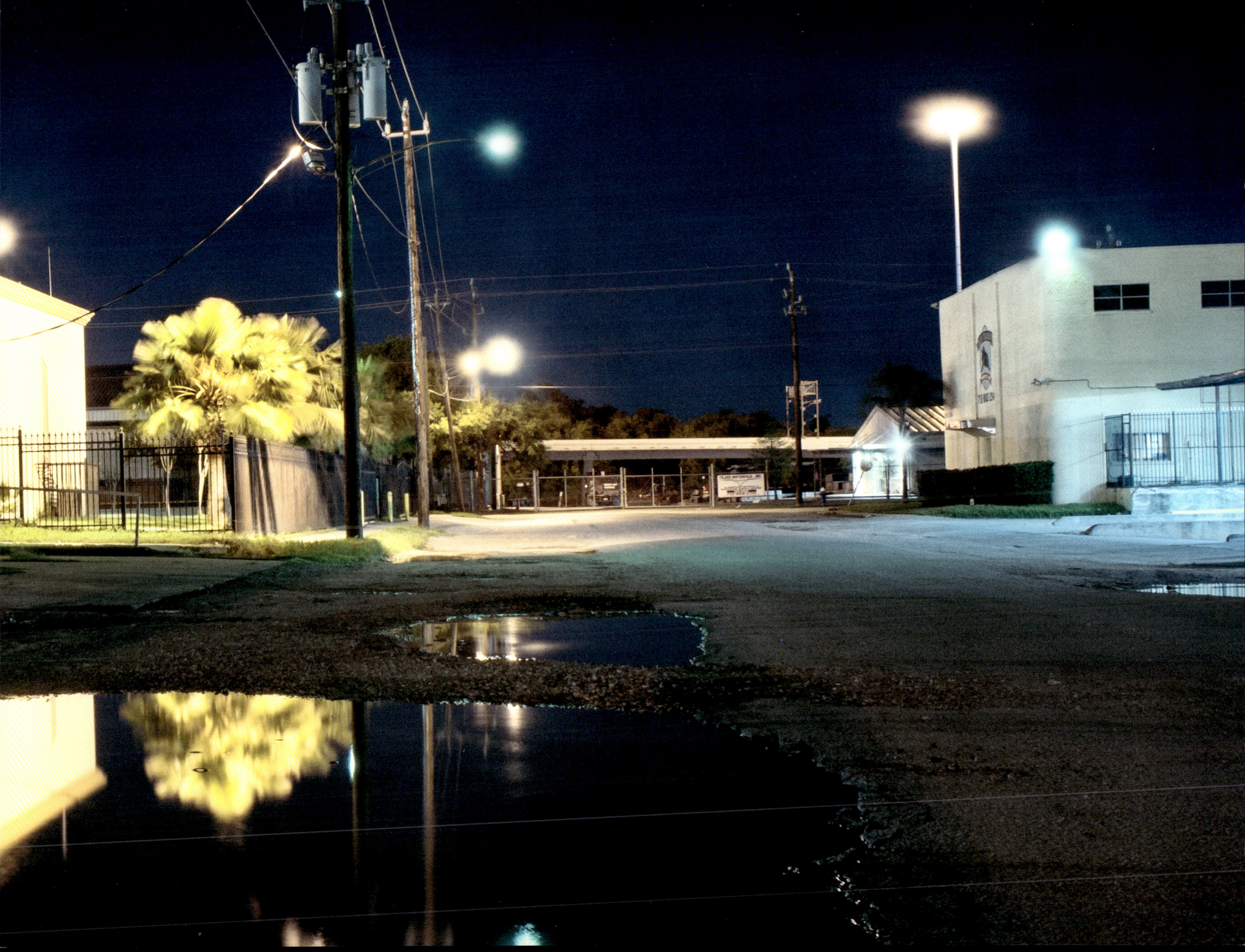

Lighted Windows, Madison Avenue, New York City

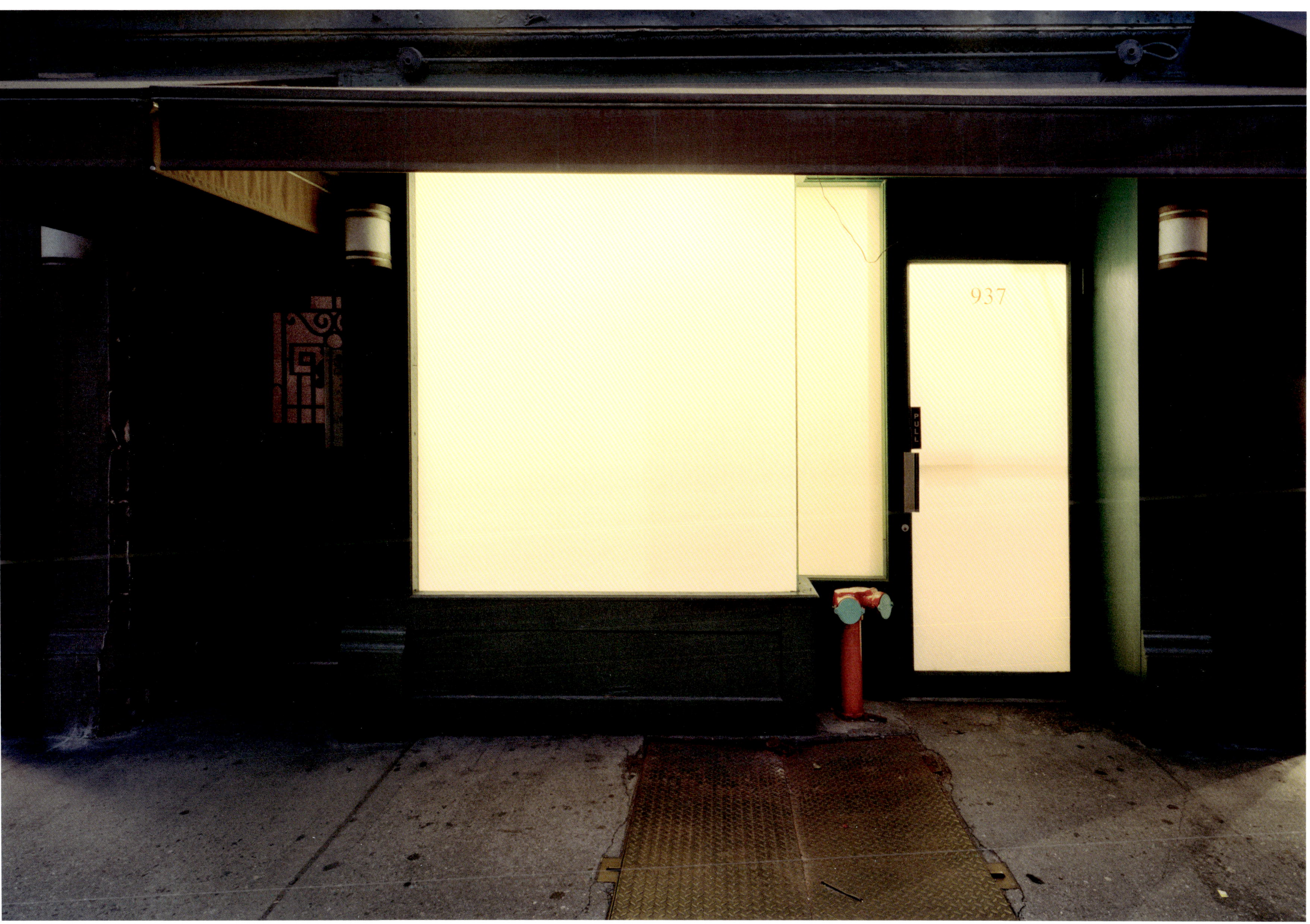
937
PULL

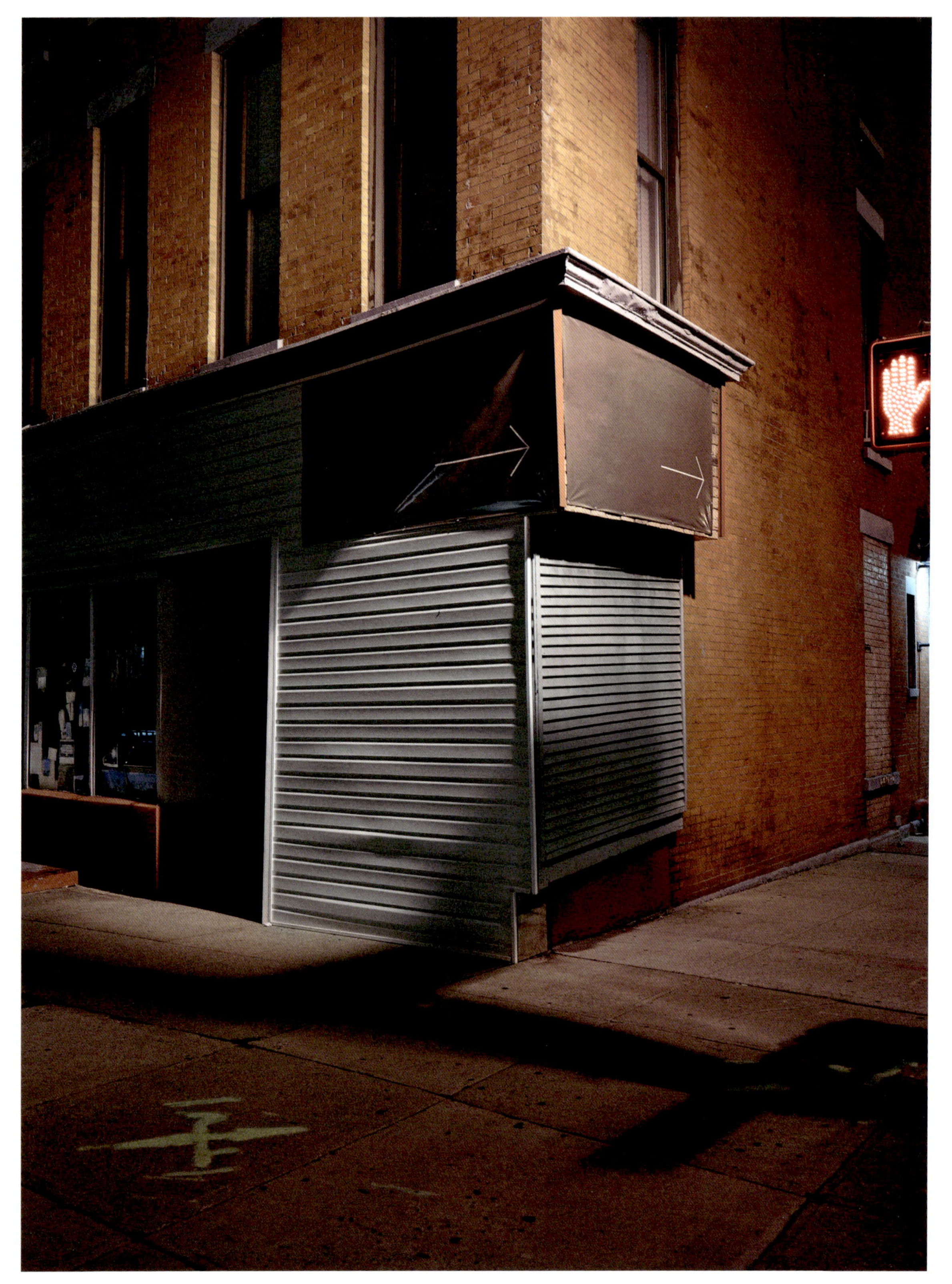

Corner, Brooklyn, New York

Opposite: Marginal Street, New York City

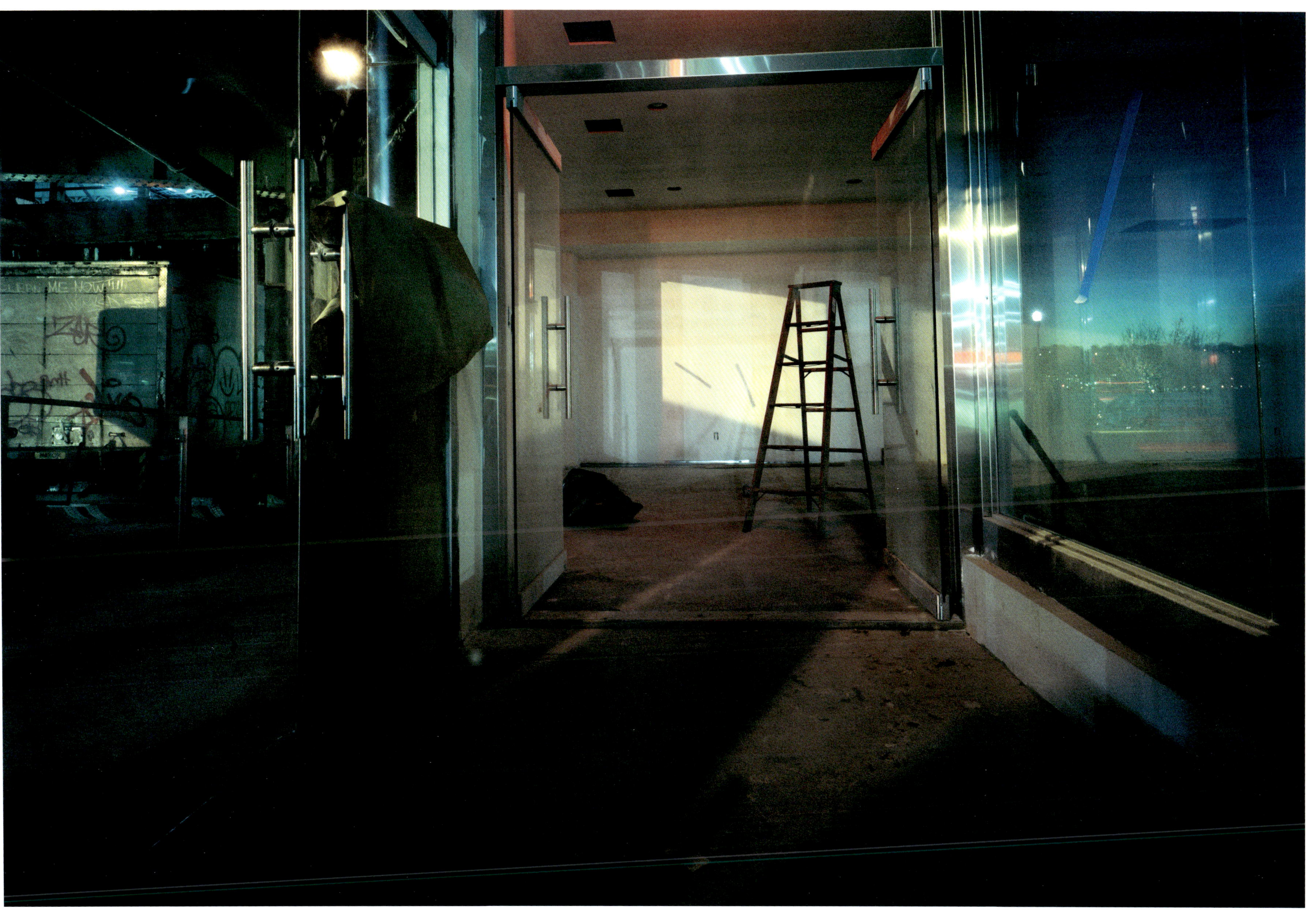

Residential Street, Detroit, Michigan

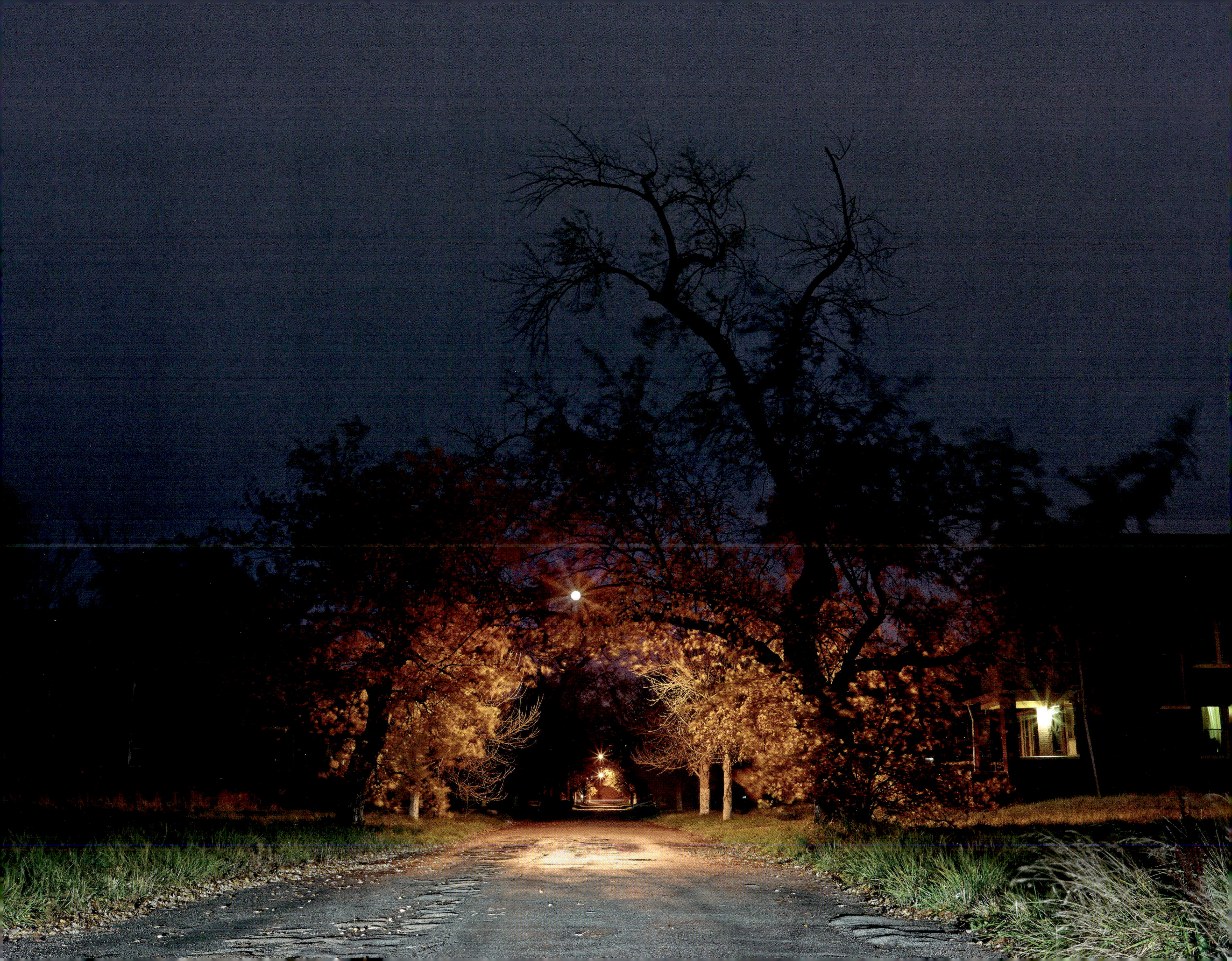

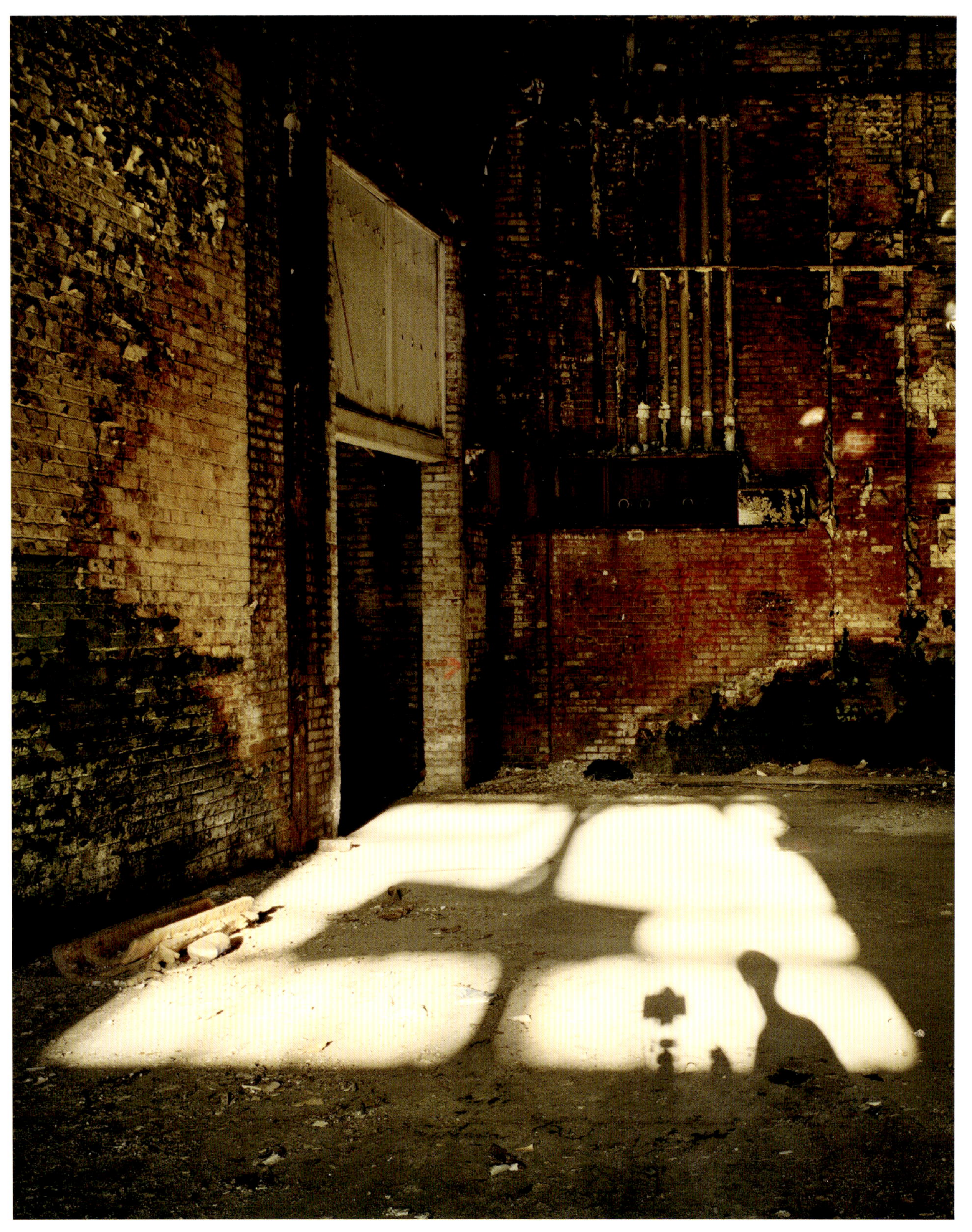

Former Warehouse, Columbus, Ohio

Opposite: Brick Wall, Newark, New Jersey

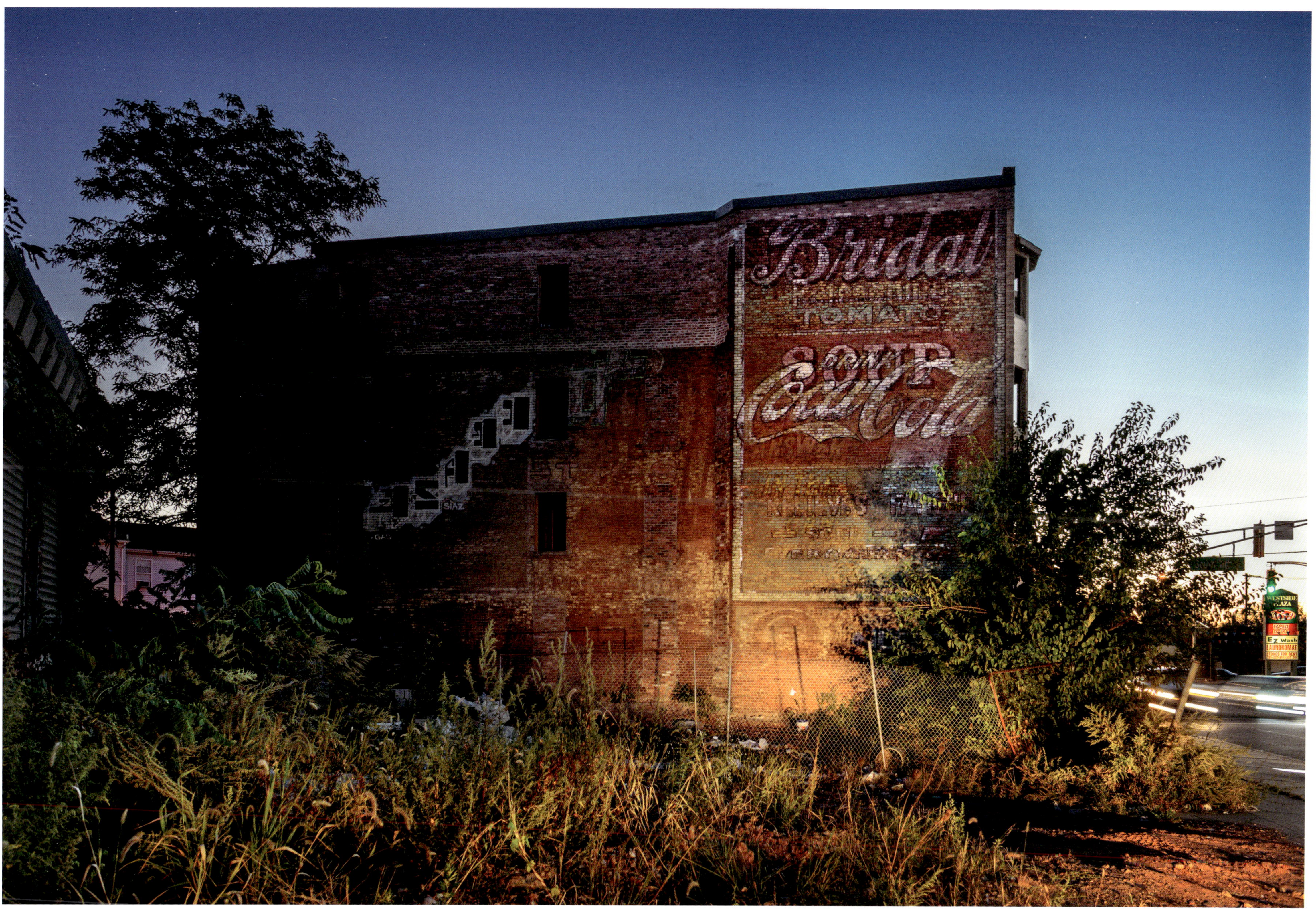
Bridal
TOMATO
SOUP
Coca Cola

Former Jack's Restaurant, Columbus, Ohio

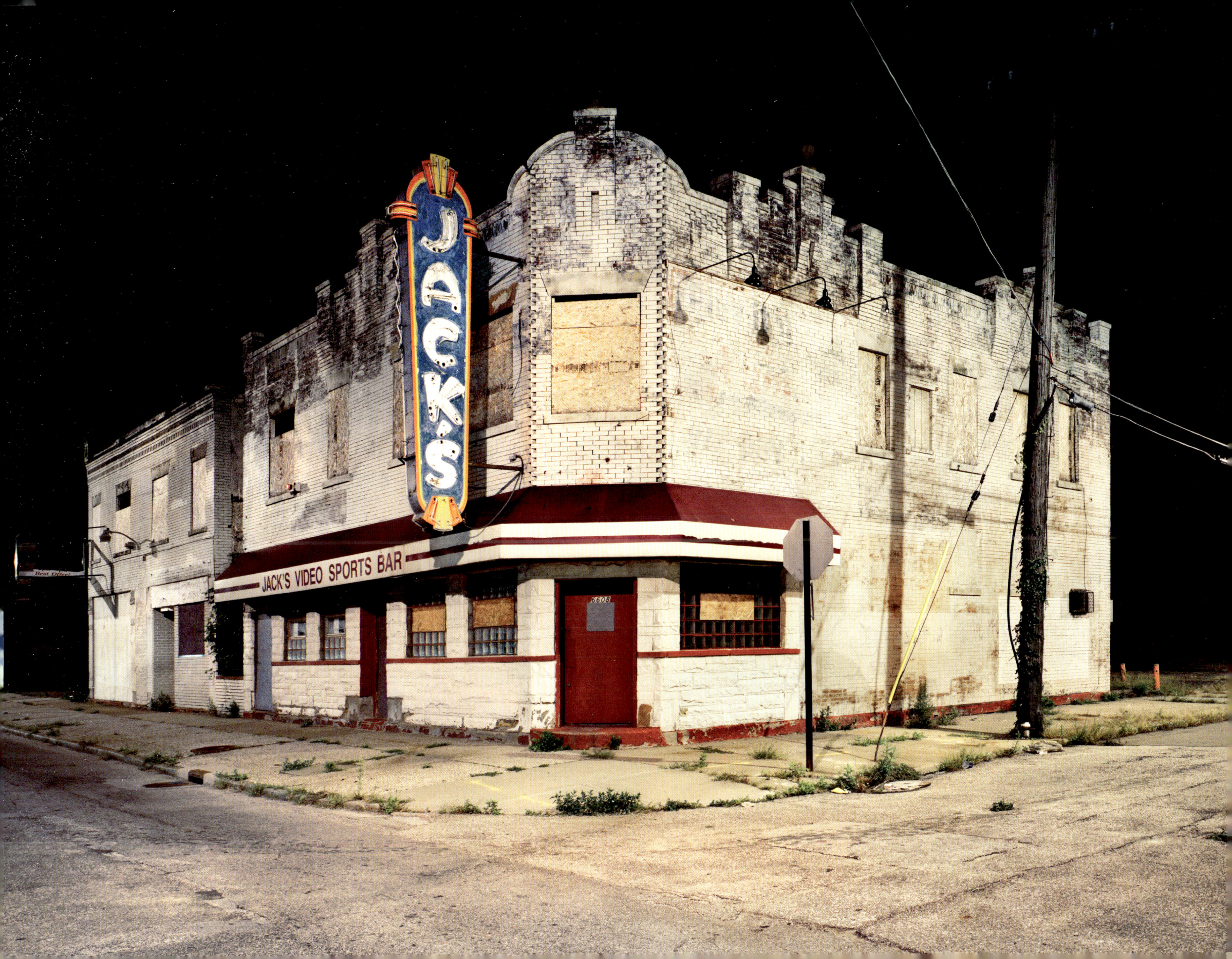

JACK'S
JACK'S VIDEO SPORTS BAR
6608
Best Offer!

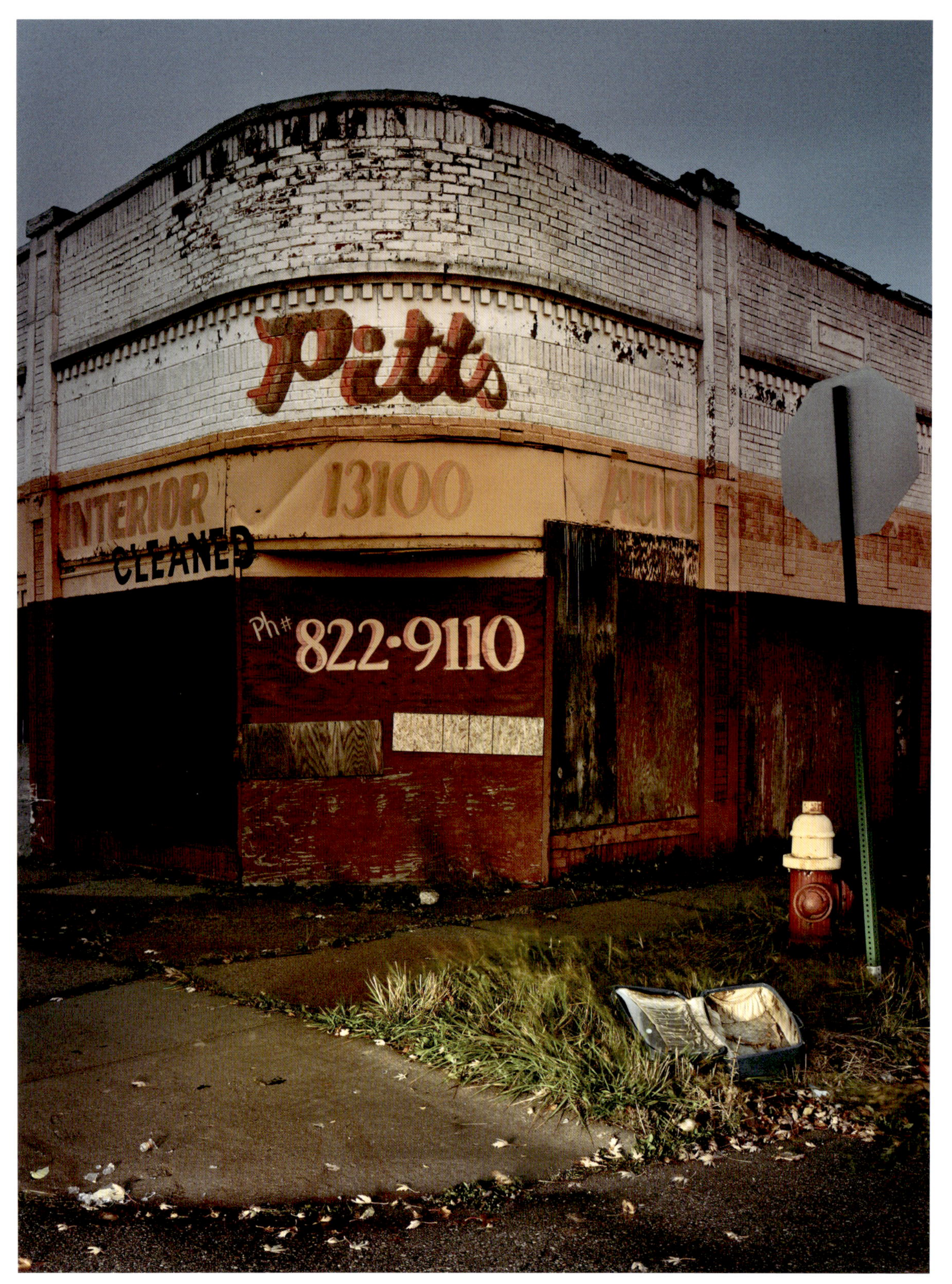

Empty Suitcase, Detroit, Michigan

Opposite: Construction Under Manhattan
Bridge, Brooklyn, New York

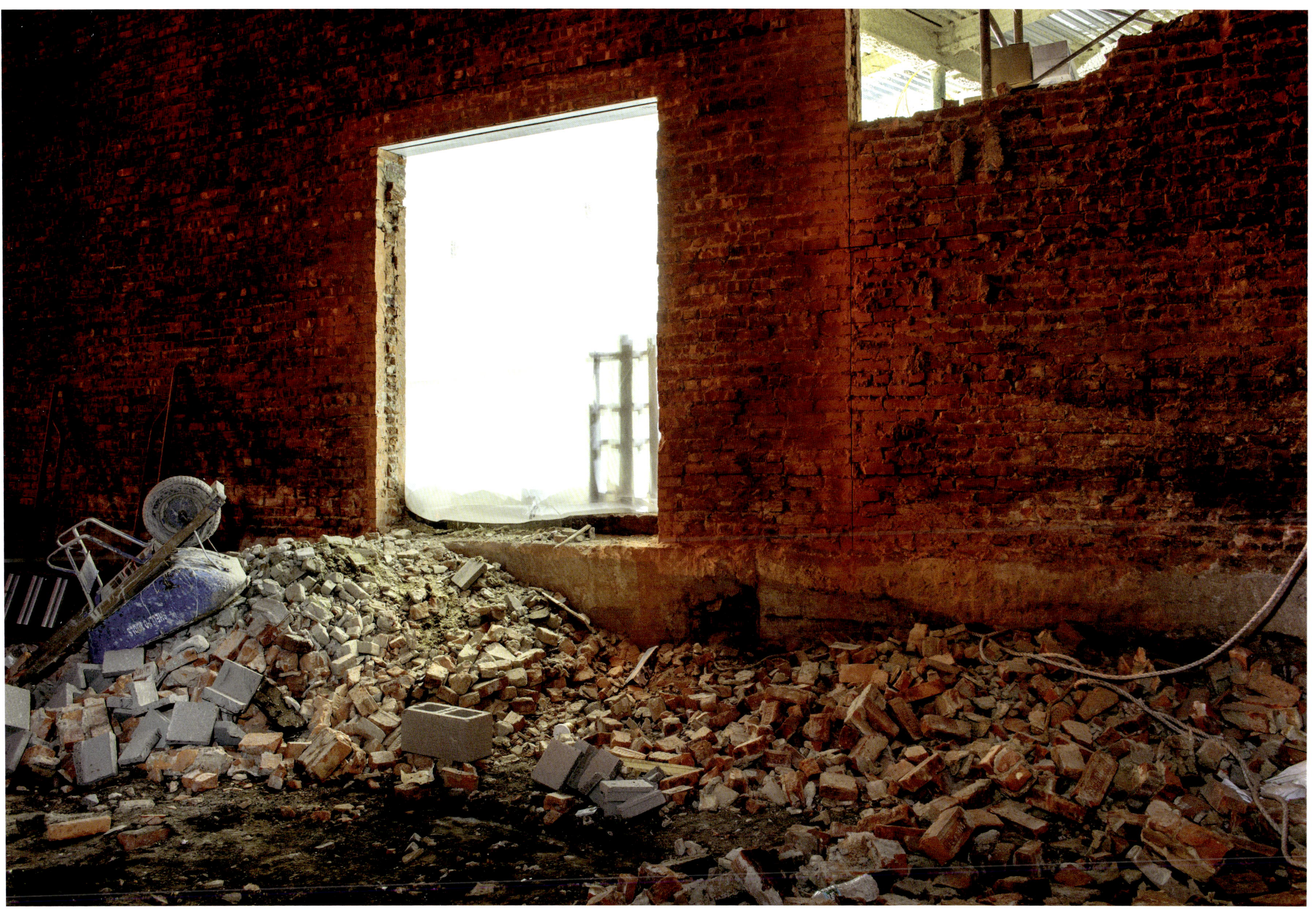

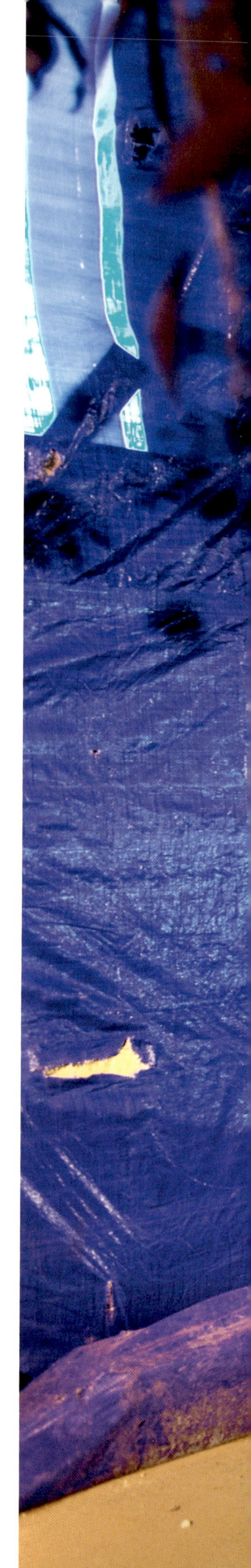

Construction, Gowanus, Brooklyn, New York

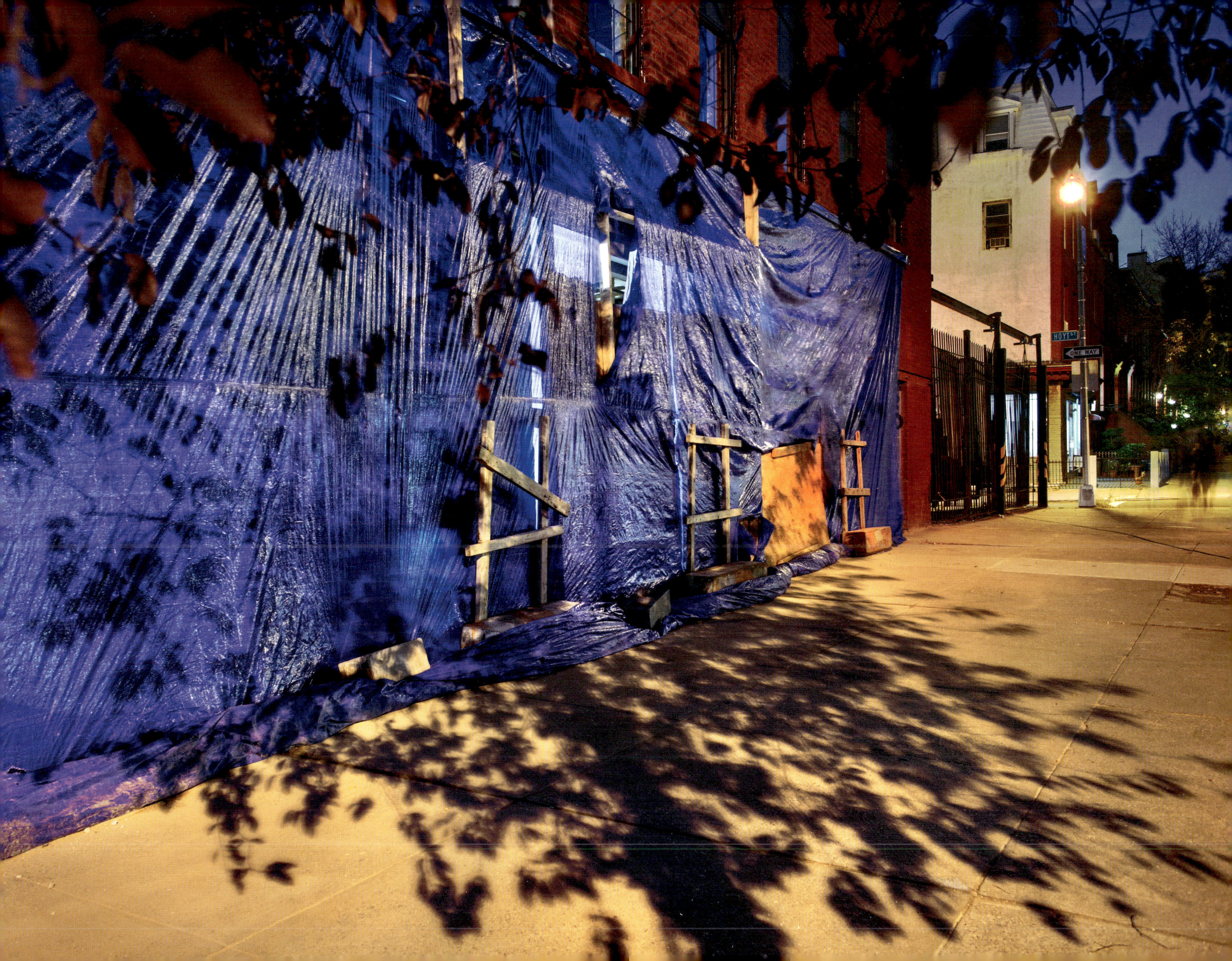
HOYT ST
ONE WAY

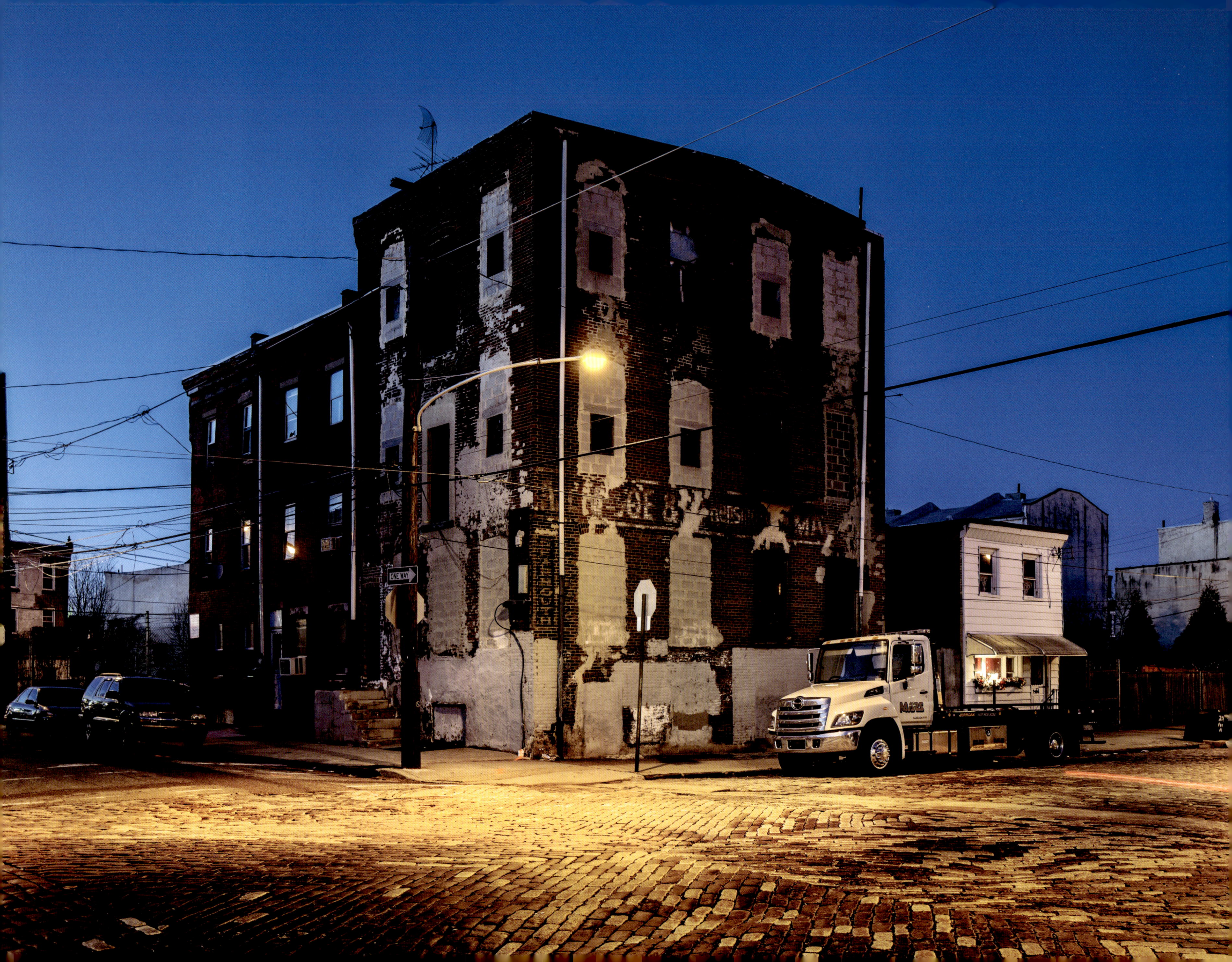

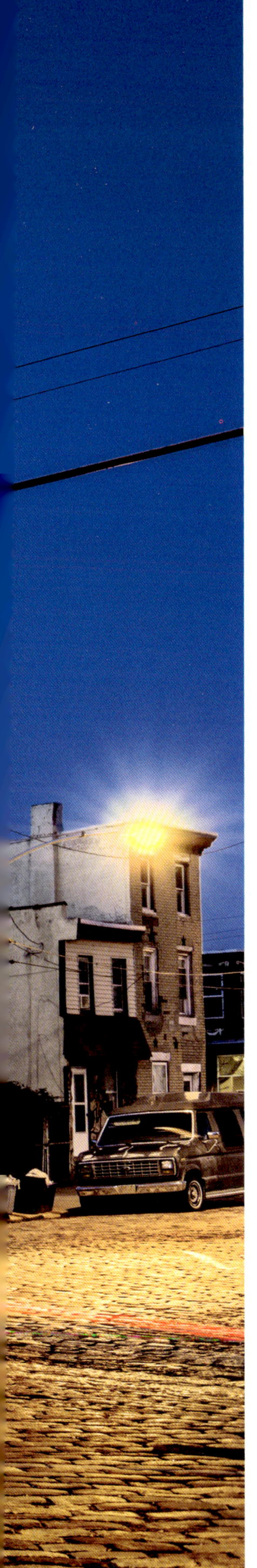

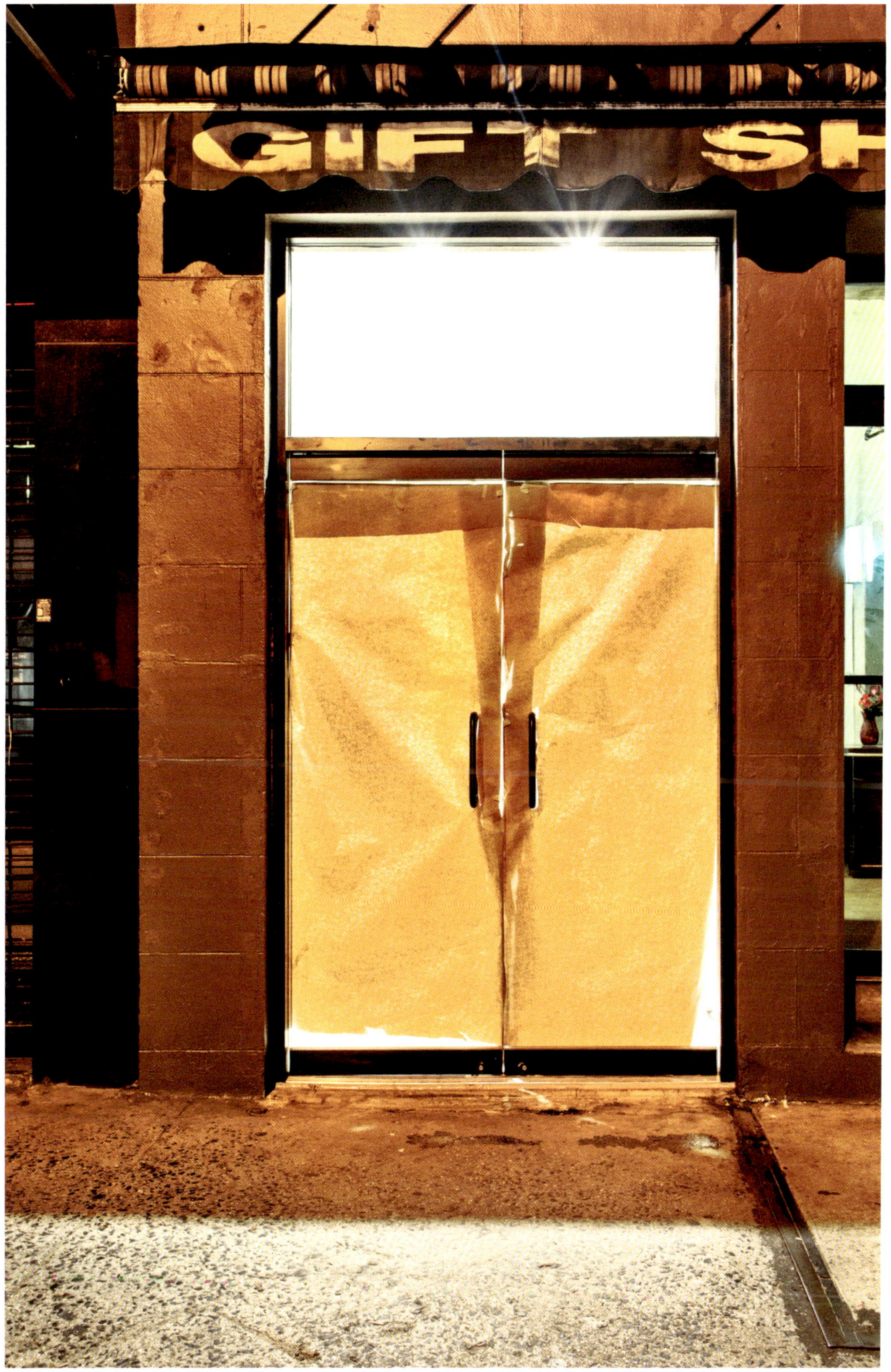

Opposite: Warehouse,
Philadelphia, Pennsylvania

East 96th Street, New York City

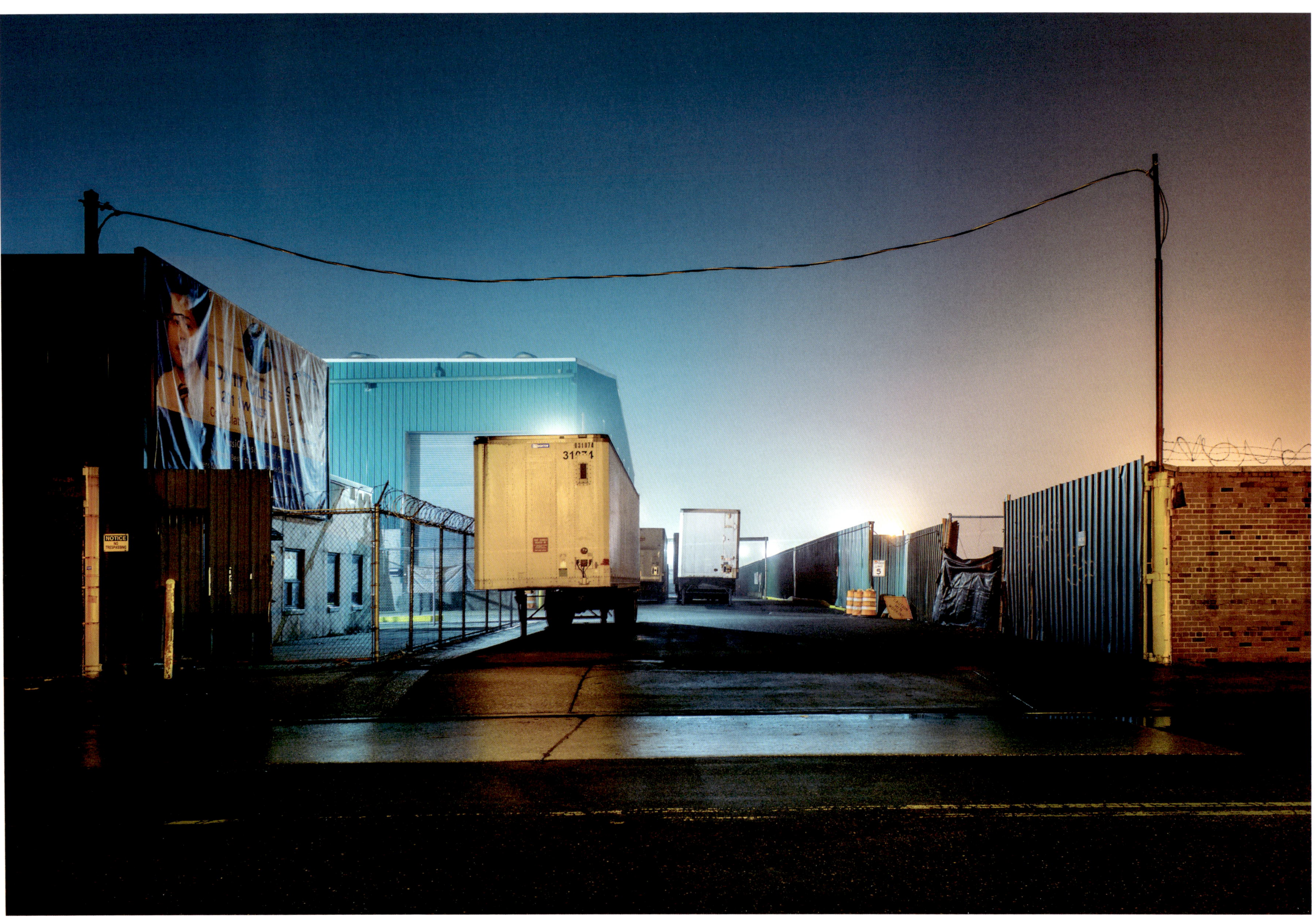

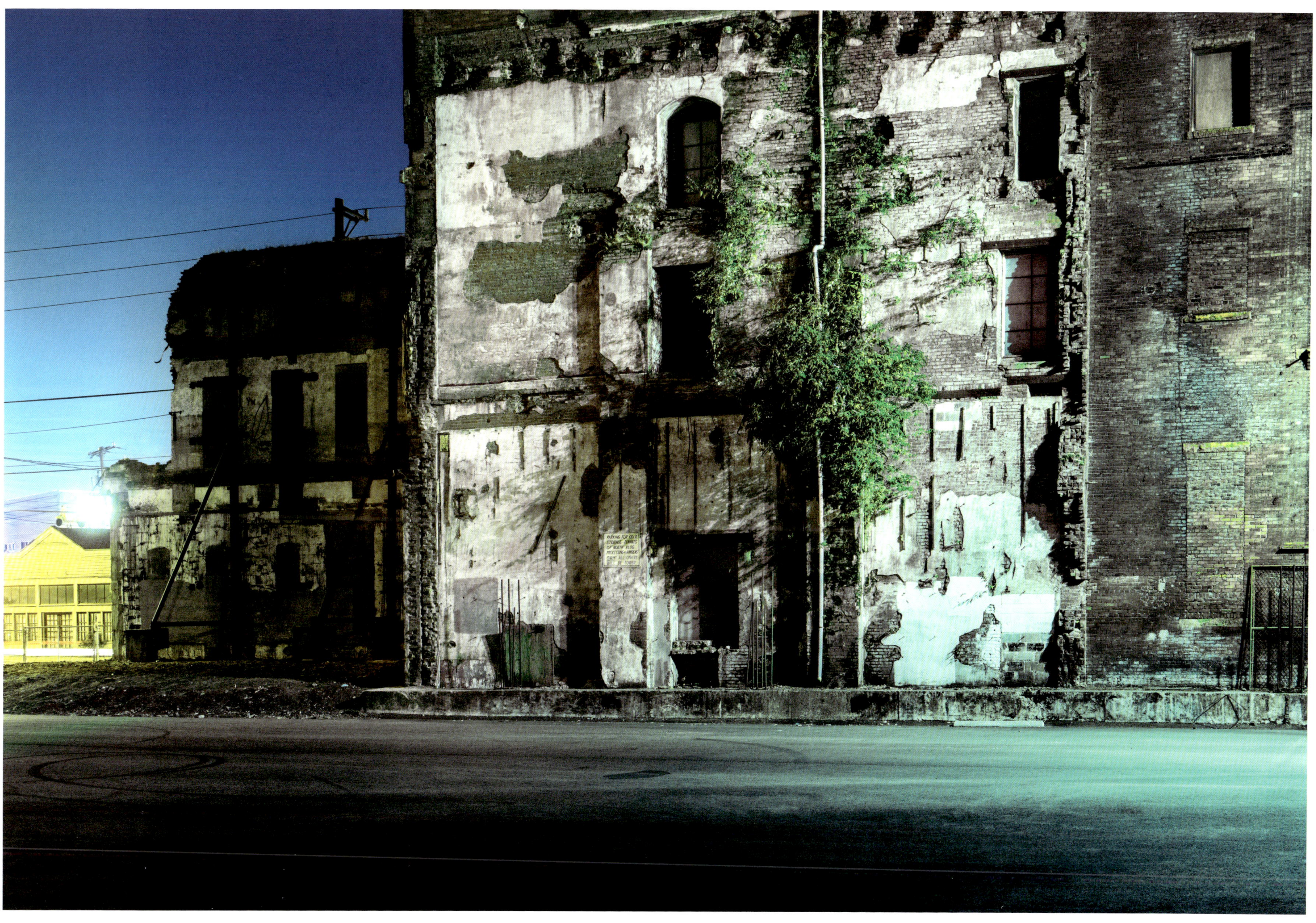
PARKING FOR COLD
STORAGE OWNERS
OF NORTH BLDG.
PFISTER & VOGEL
DEPT. ALL OTHERS
BE TOWED

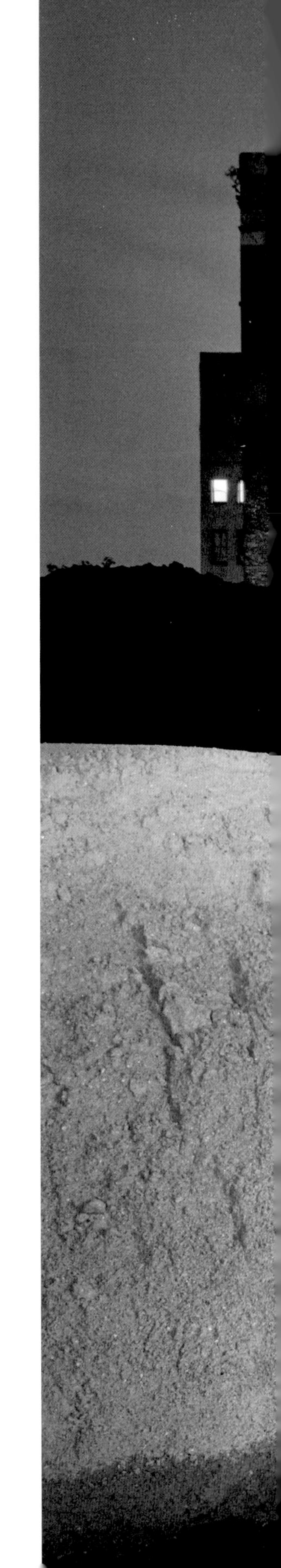

Page 98: Parking Lot, Bushwick, Brooklyn, New York

Page 99: Warehouse, Seattle, Washington

Park Construction Under Manhattan Bridge, Brooklyn, New York

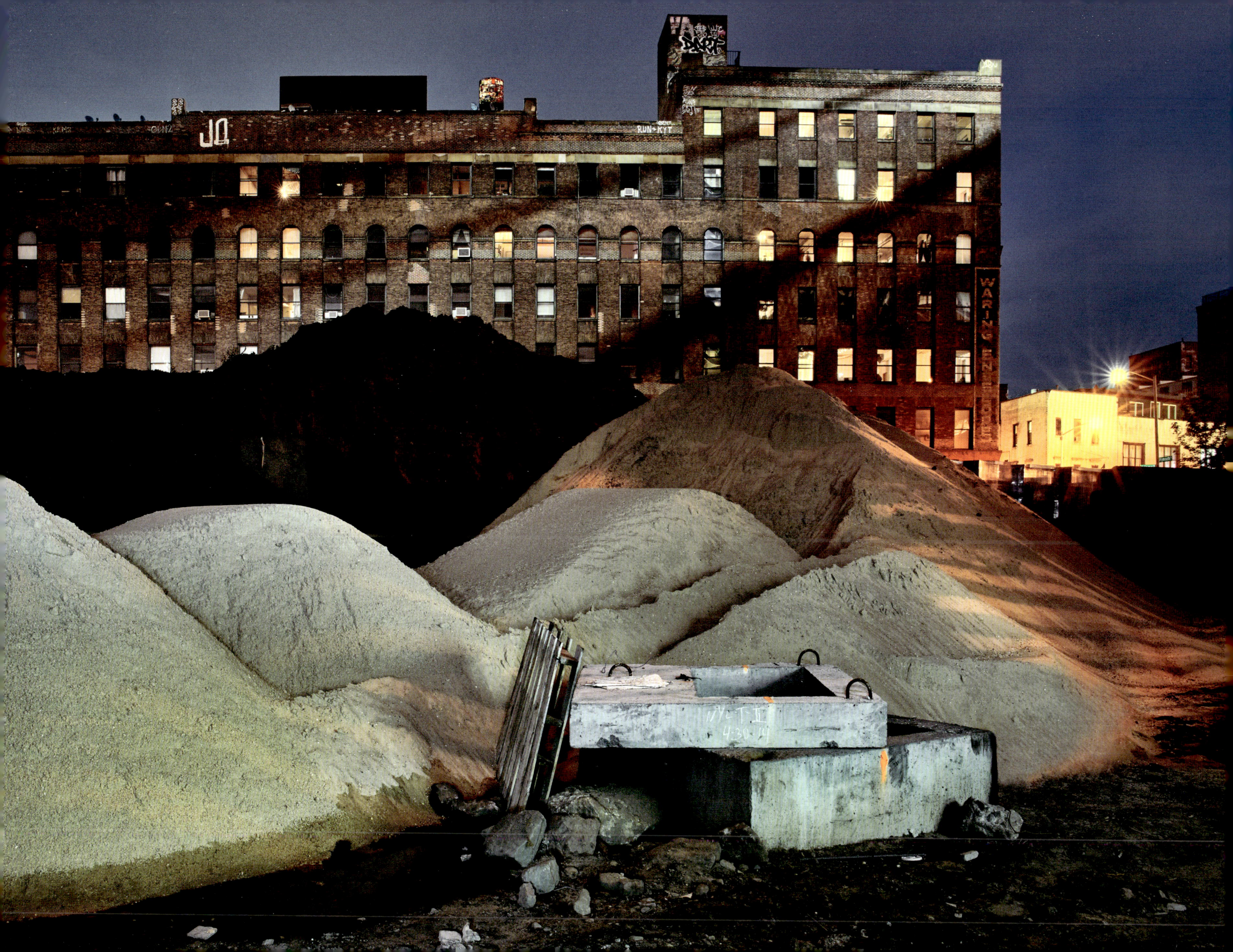

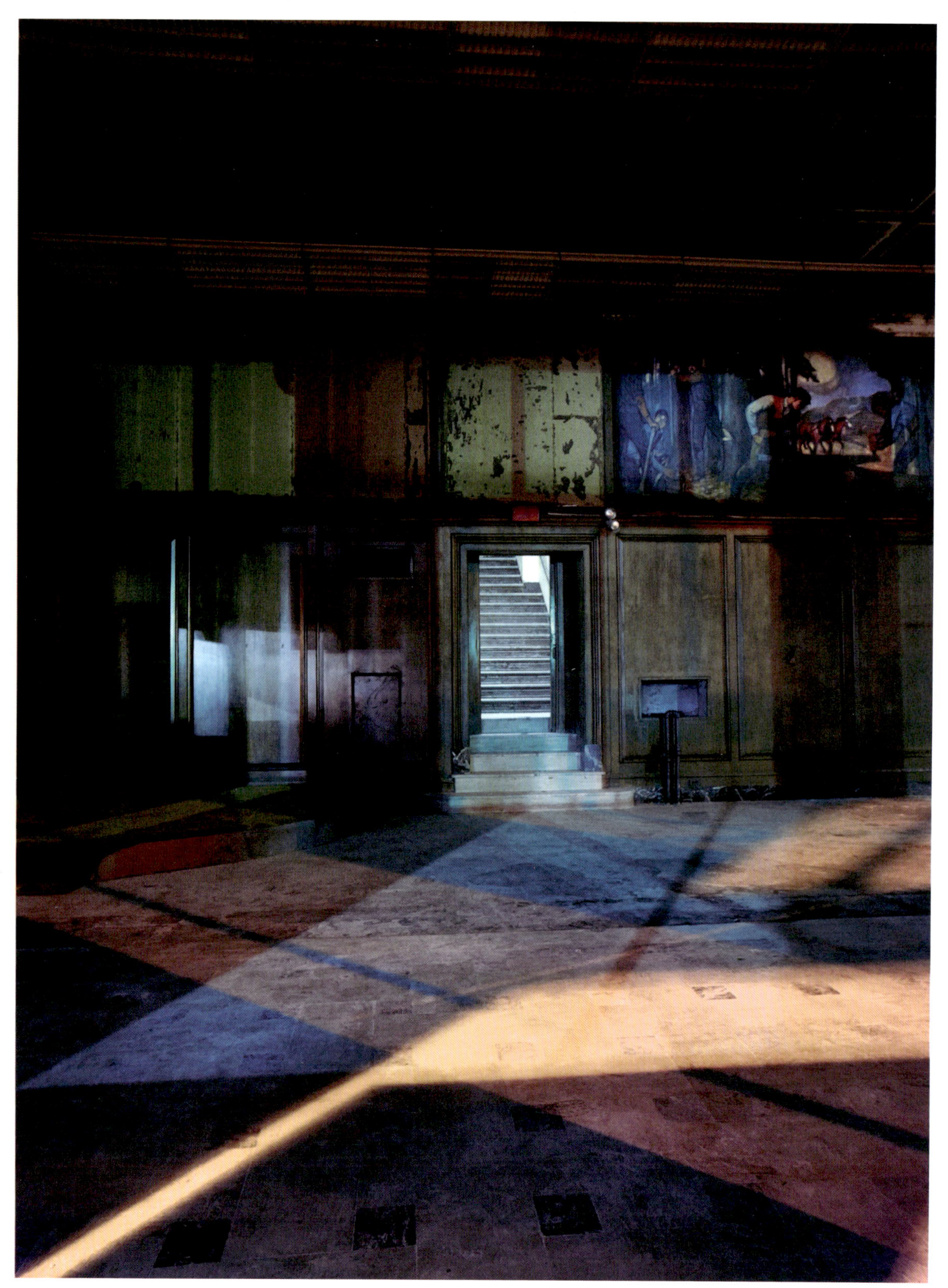

Former Lobby, Detroit, Michigan

Opposite: Warehouse, Los Angeles, California

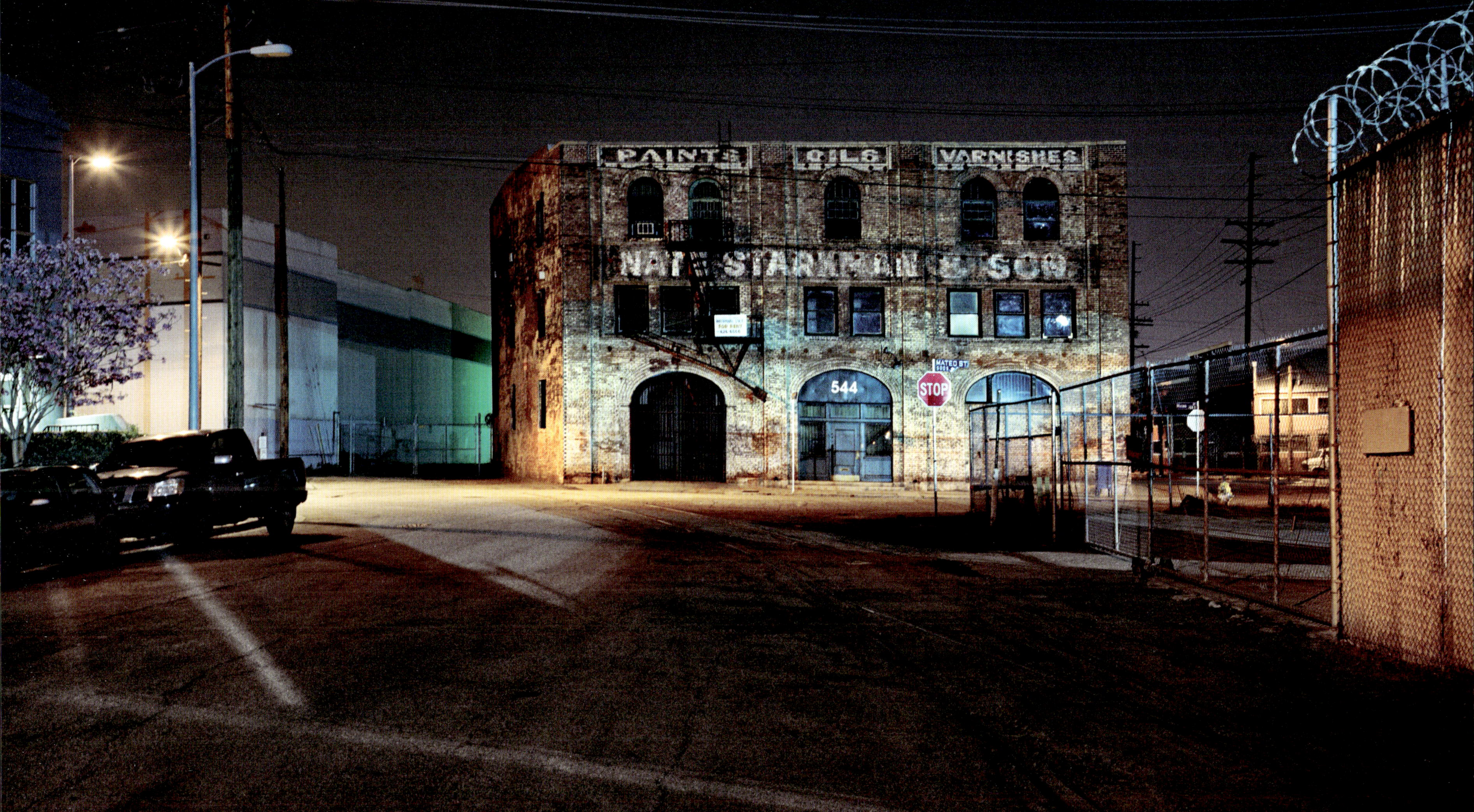

PAINTS   OILS   VARNISHES
NAT STARKMAN & SON
544
STOP

Former Clothing Store, Columbus Avenue, New York City

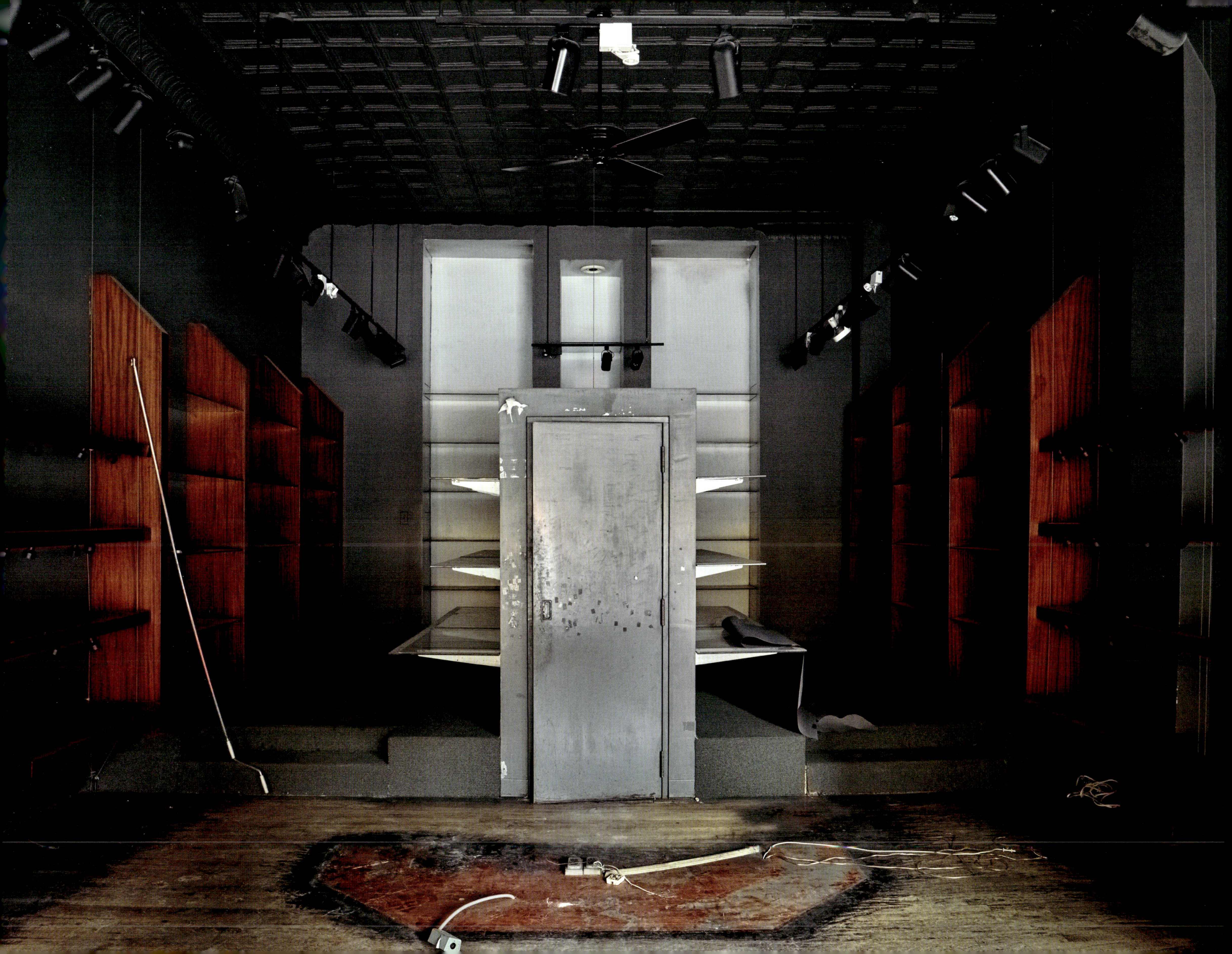

Warehouse, Newburgh, New York

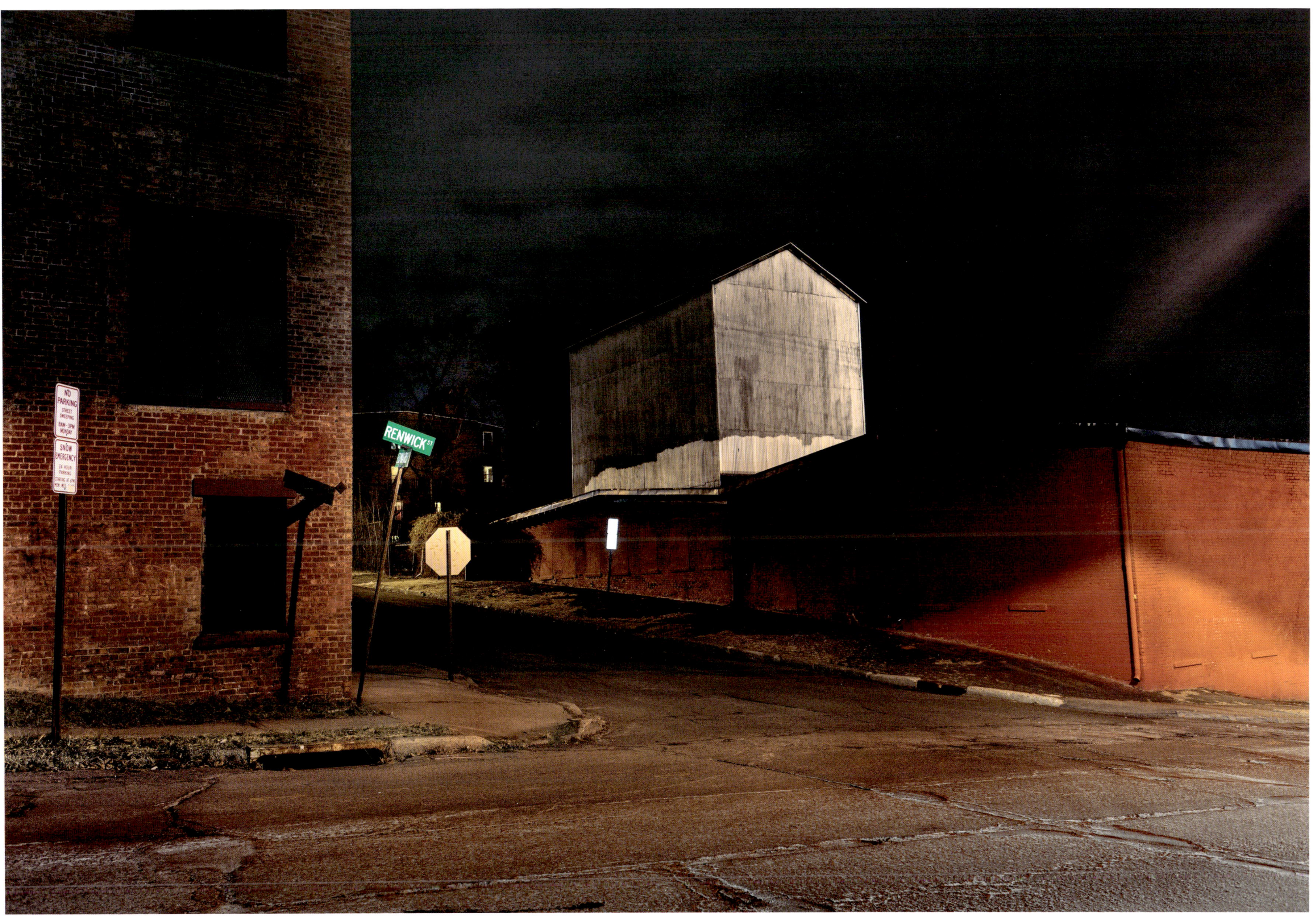

RENWICK ST
NO PARKING
SNOW EMERGENCY

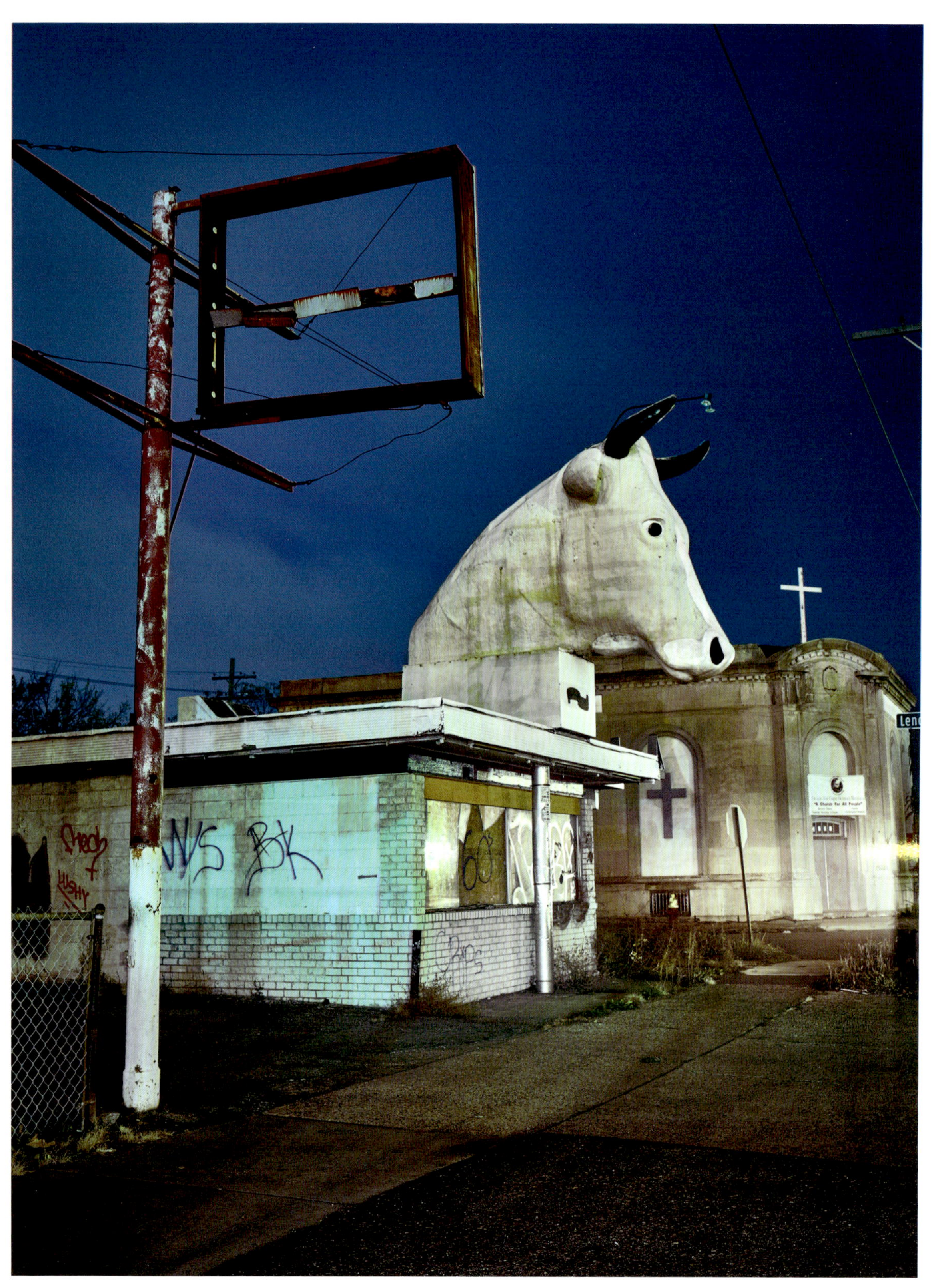

Former Ice Cream Shop, Detroit, Michigan

Opposite: Parking Garage, Detroit, Michigan

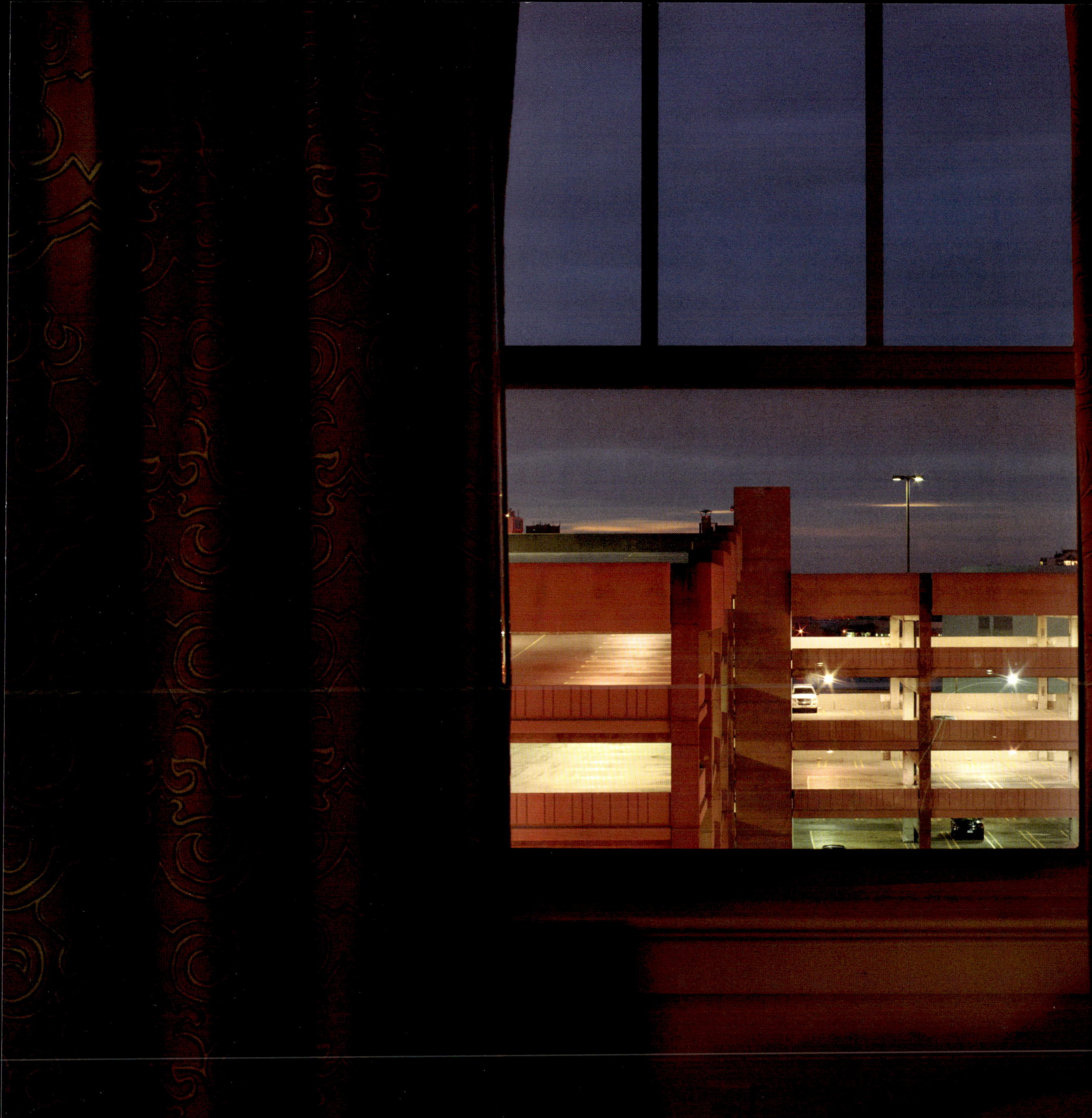

Empty Store, 42nd Street and 6th Avenue, New York City

Page 112: Garage, Baltimore, Maryland

Page 113: Riverside Drive, New York City

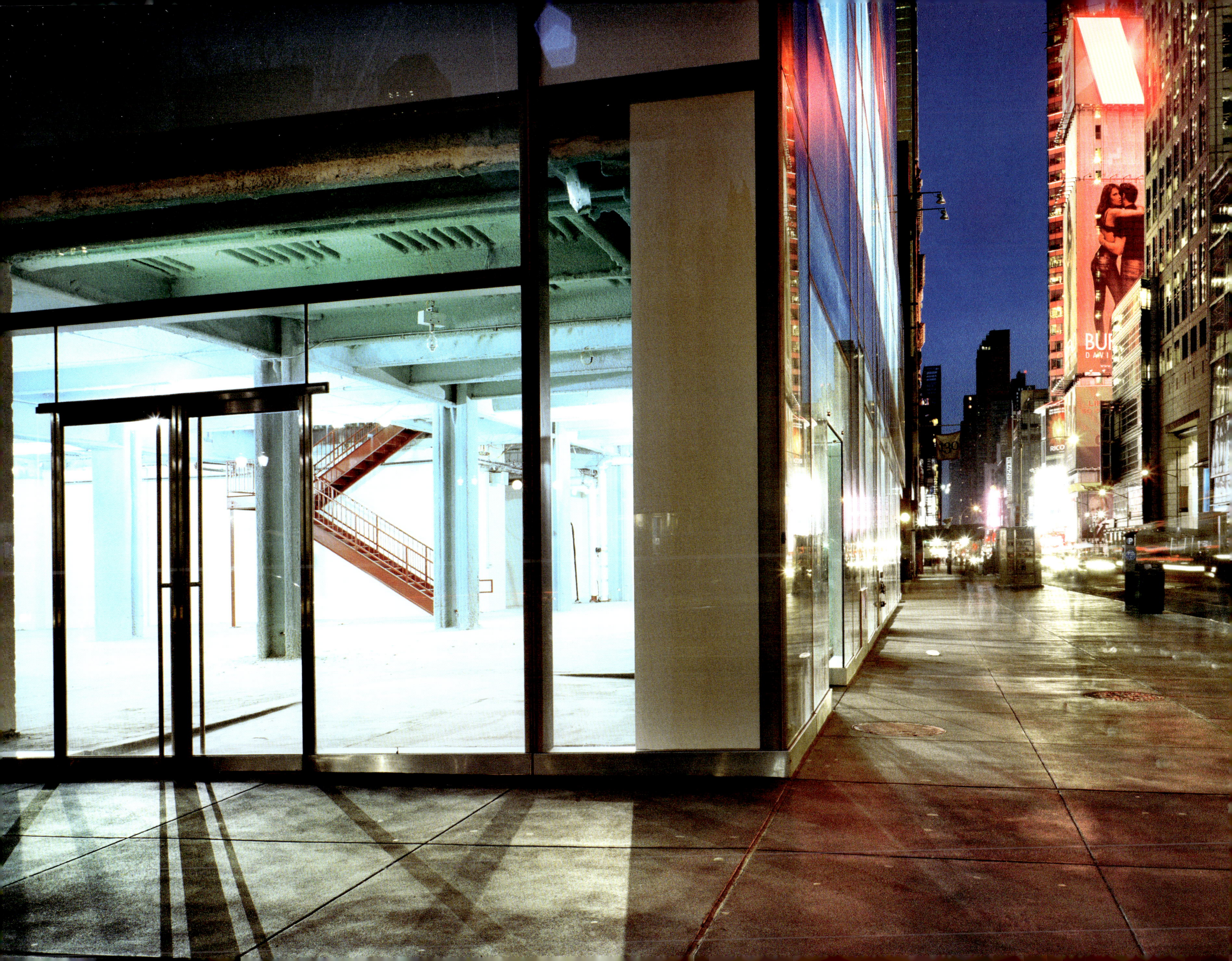

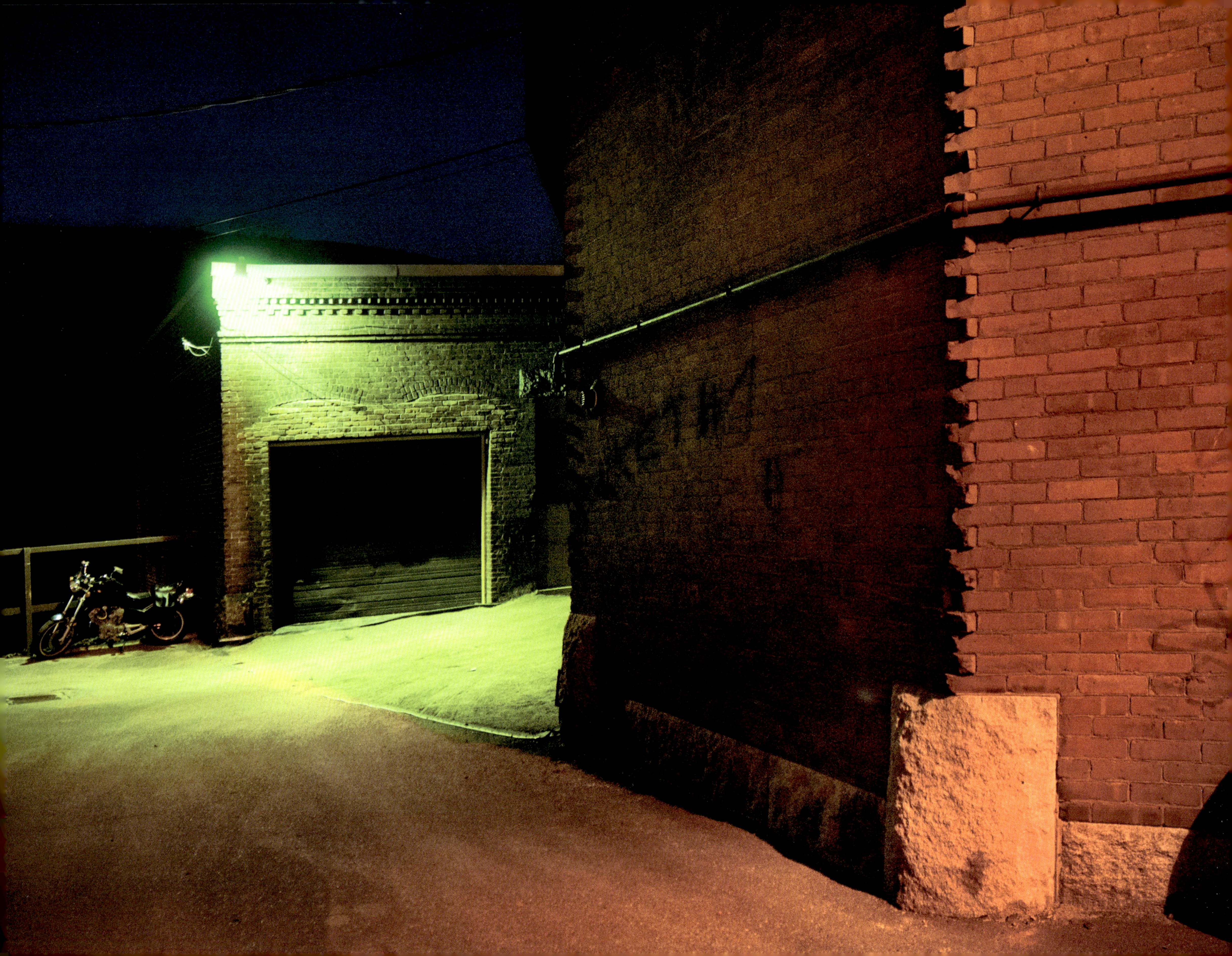

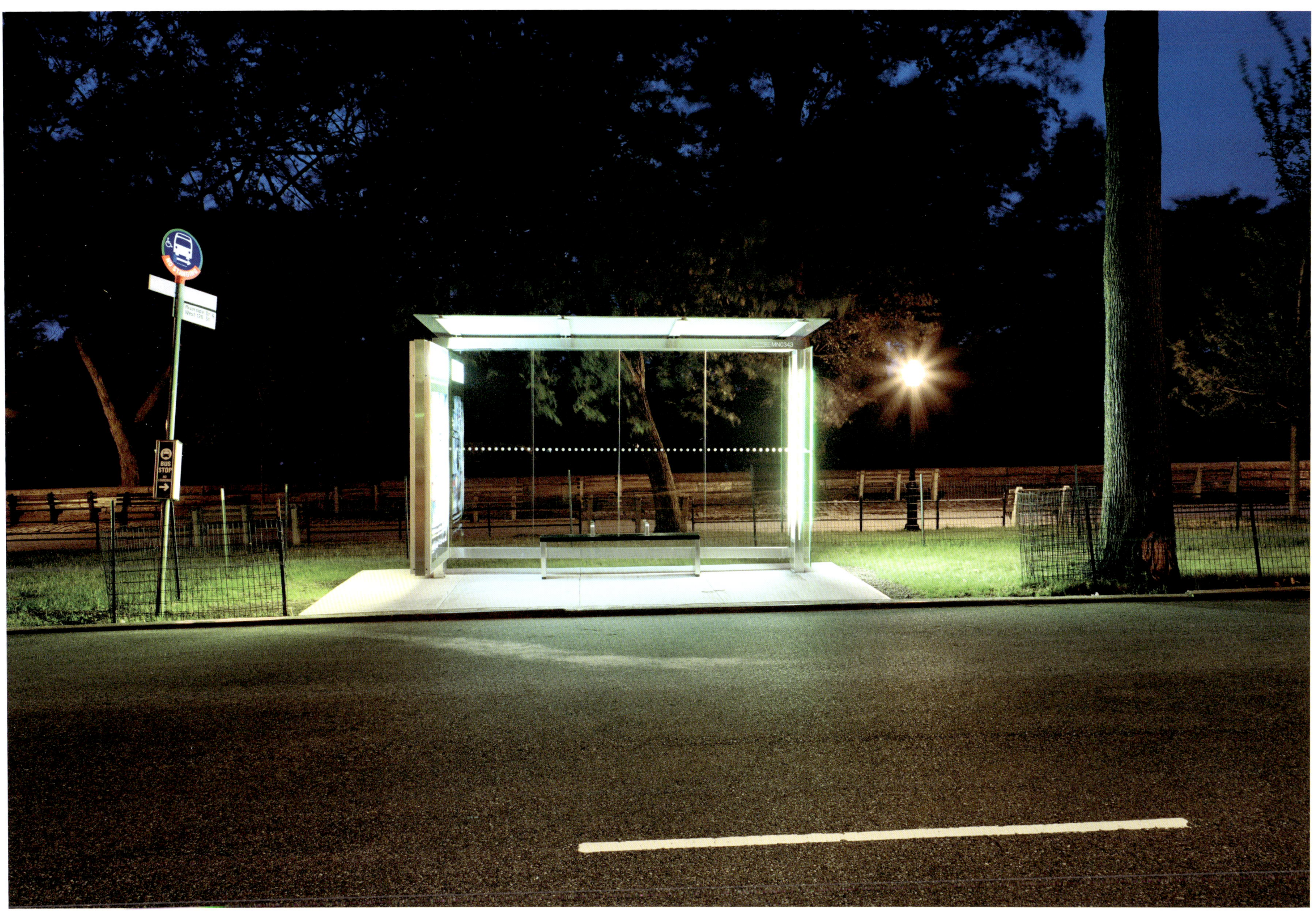

Closed Café, Detroit, Michigan

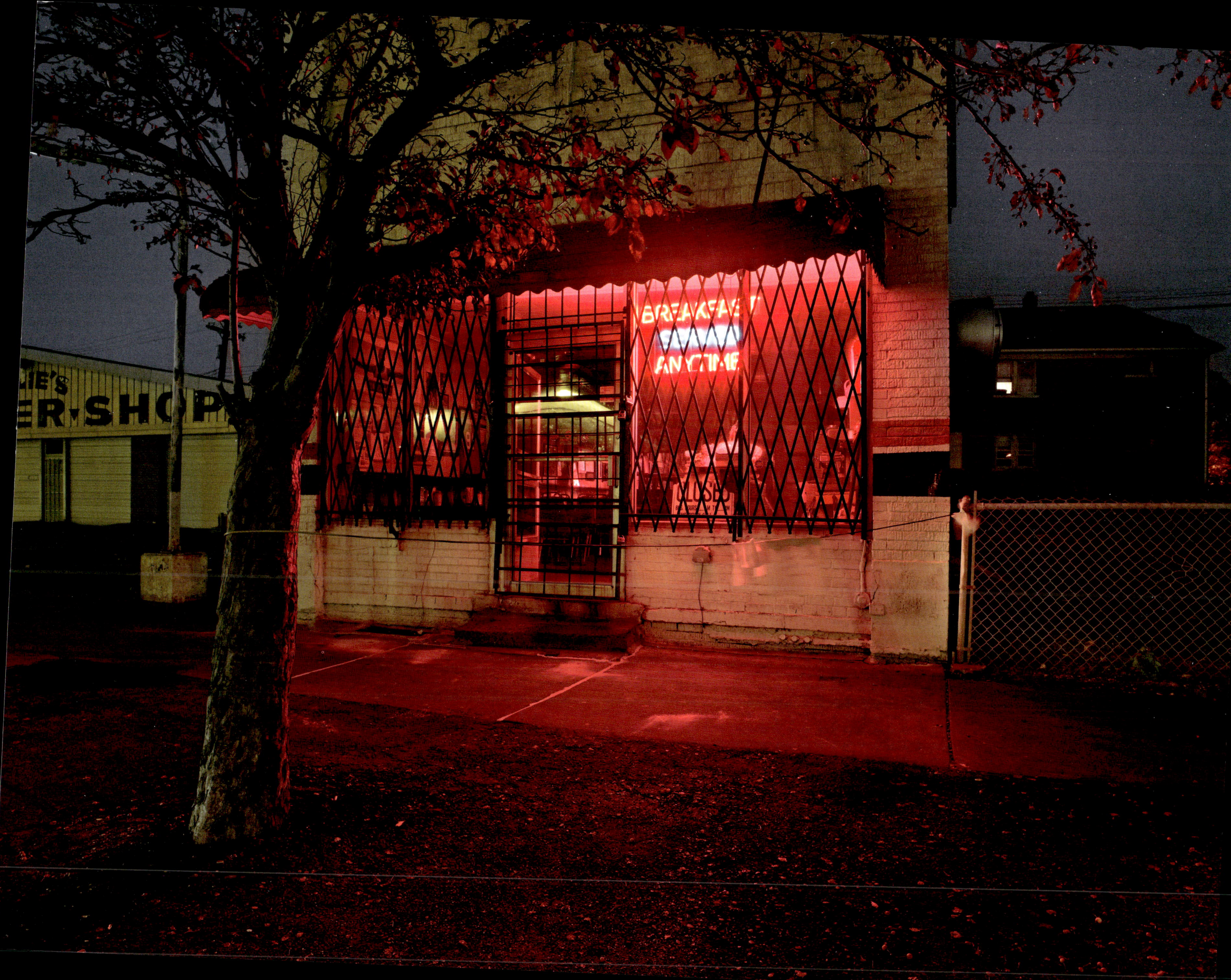
BREAKFAST
ANYTIME
IE'S
ER·SHOP

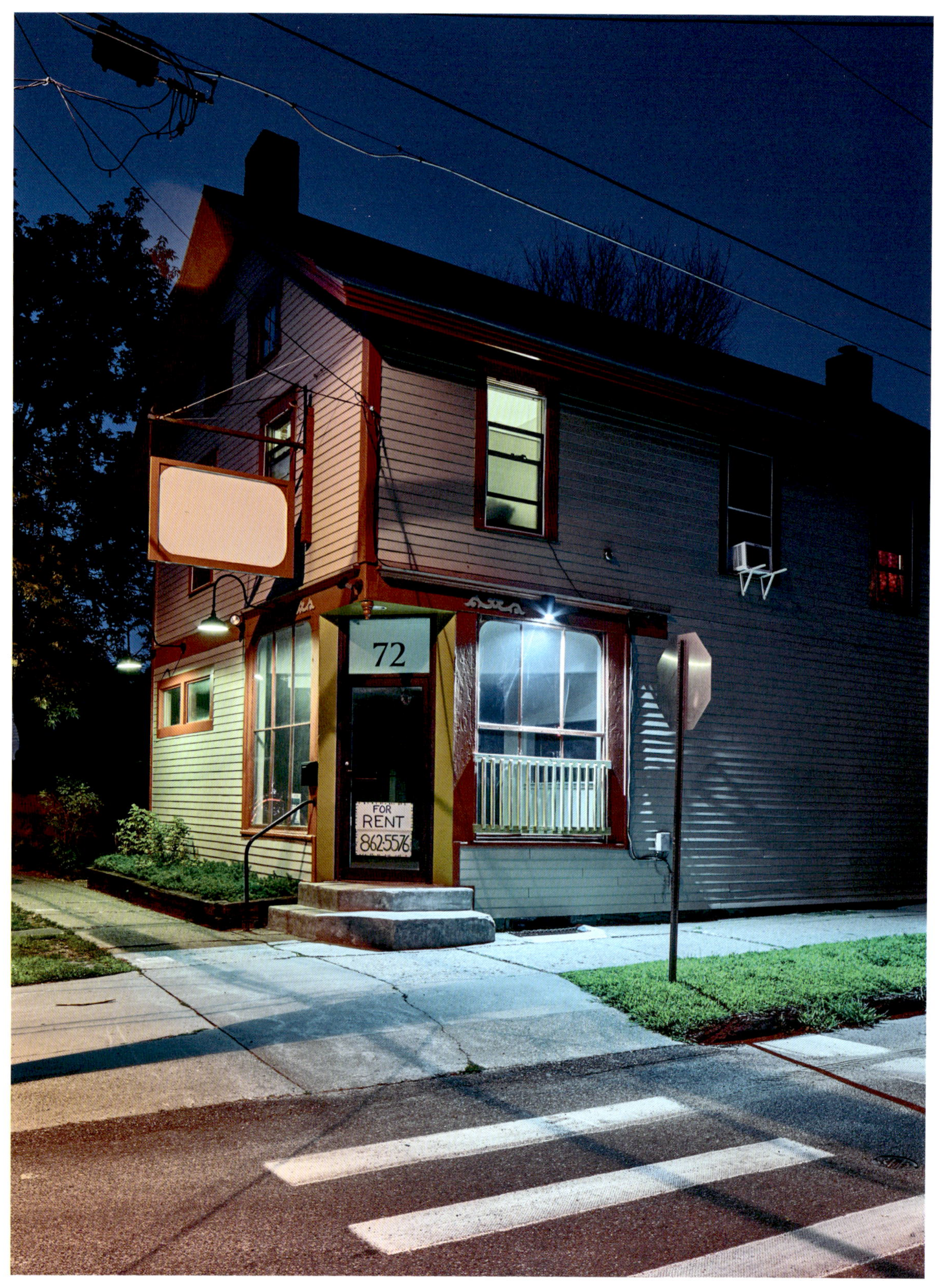

Corner Store, Burlington, Vermont

Opposite: Gowanus Canal, Brooklyn, New York

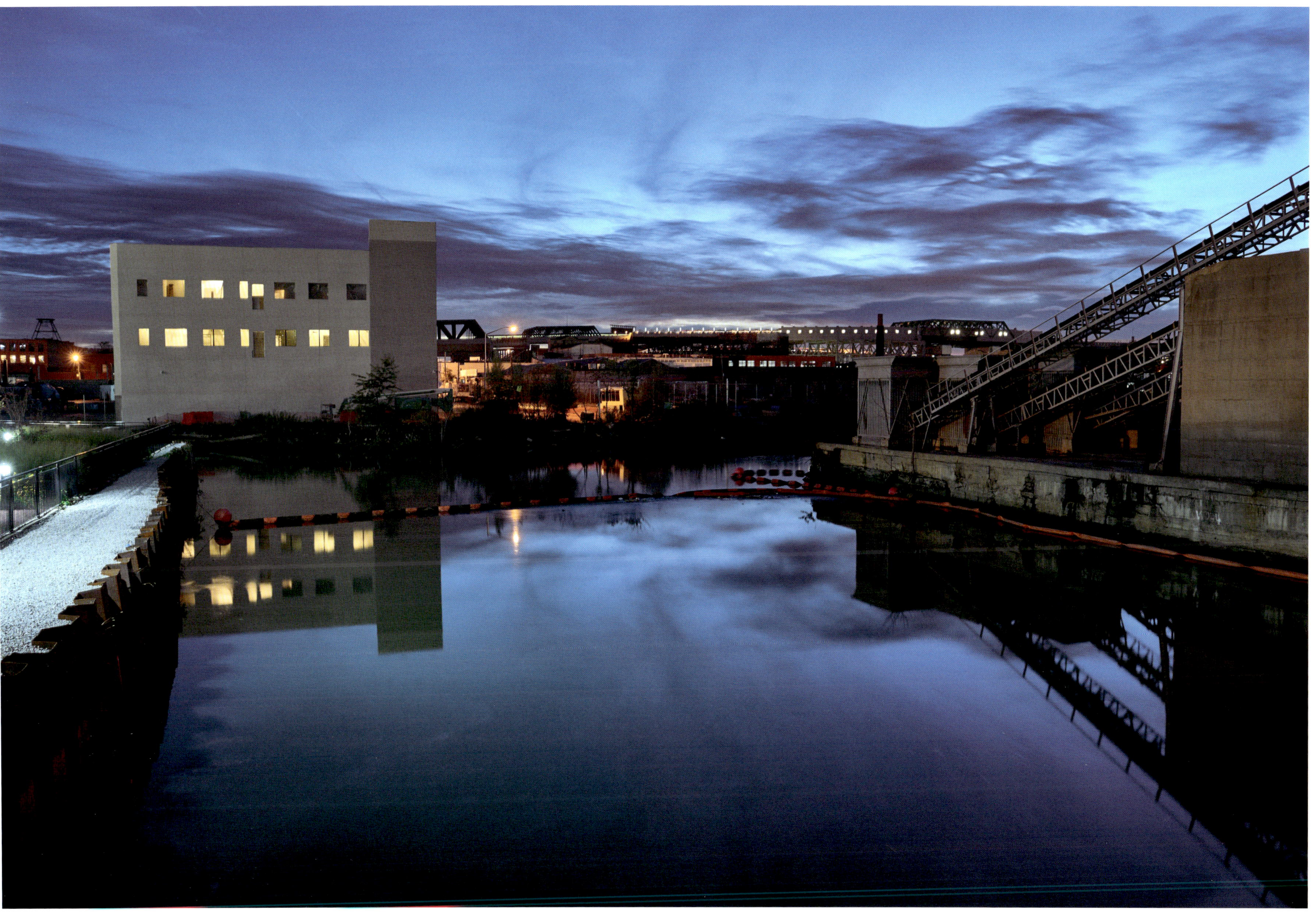

Parking Garage, Houston, Texas

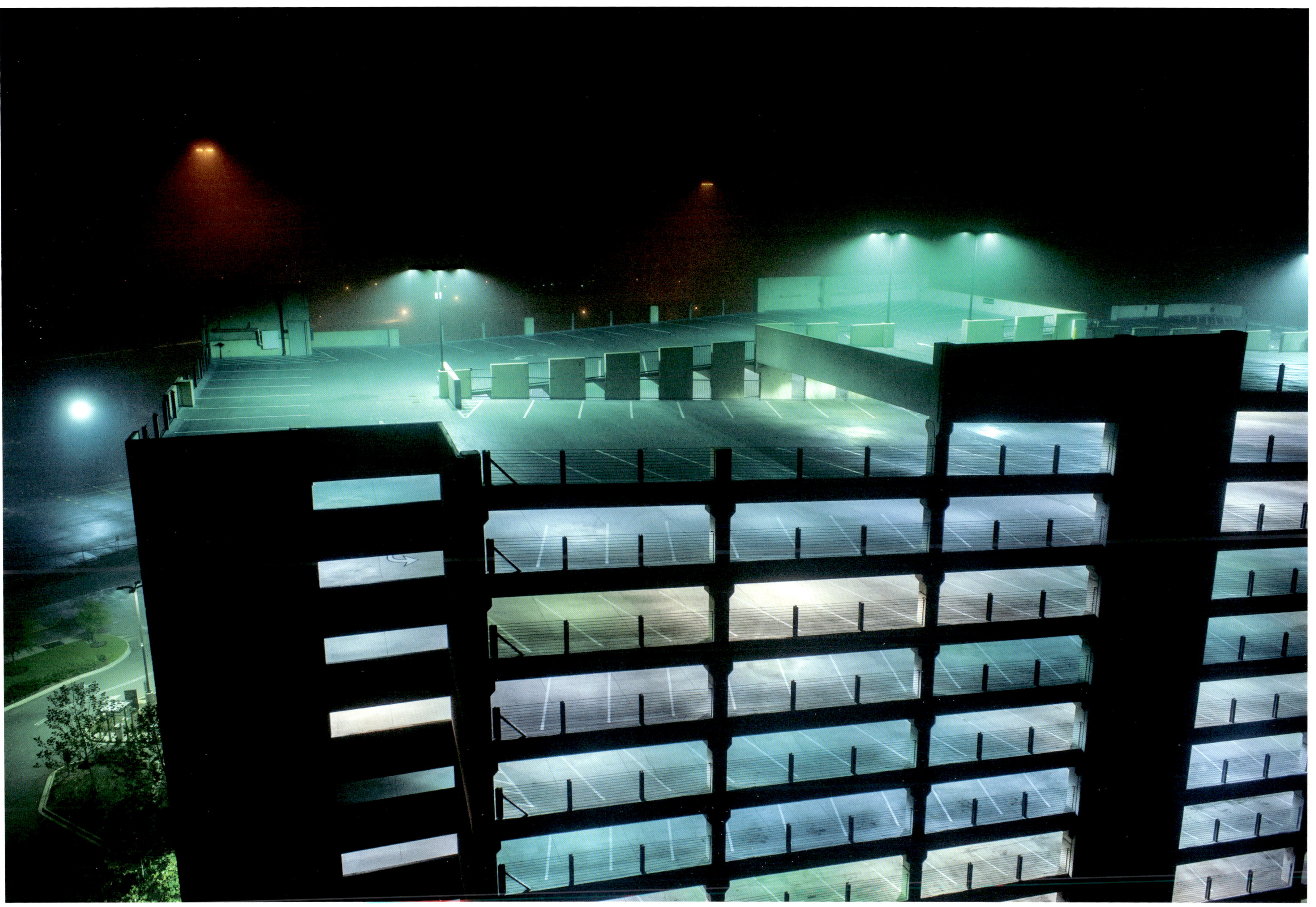

Dyckman Street, Red Hook, Brooklyn, New York

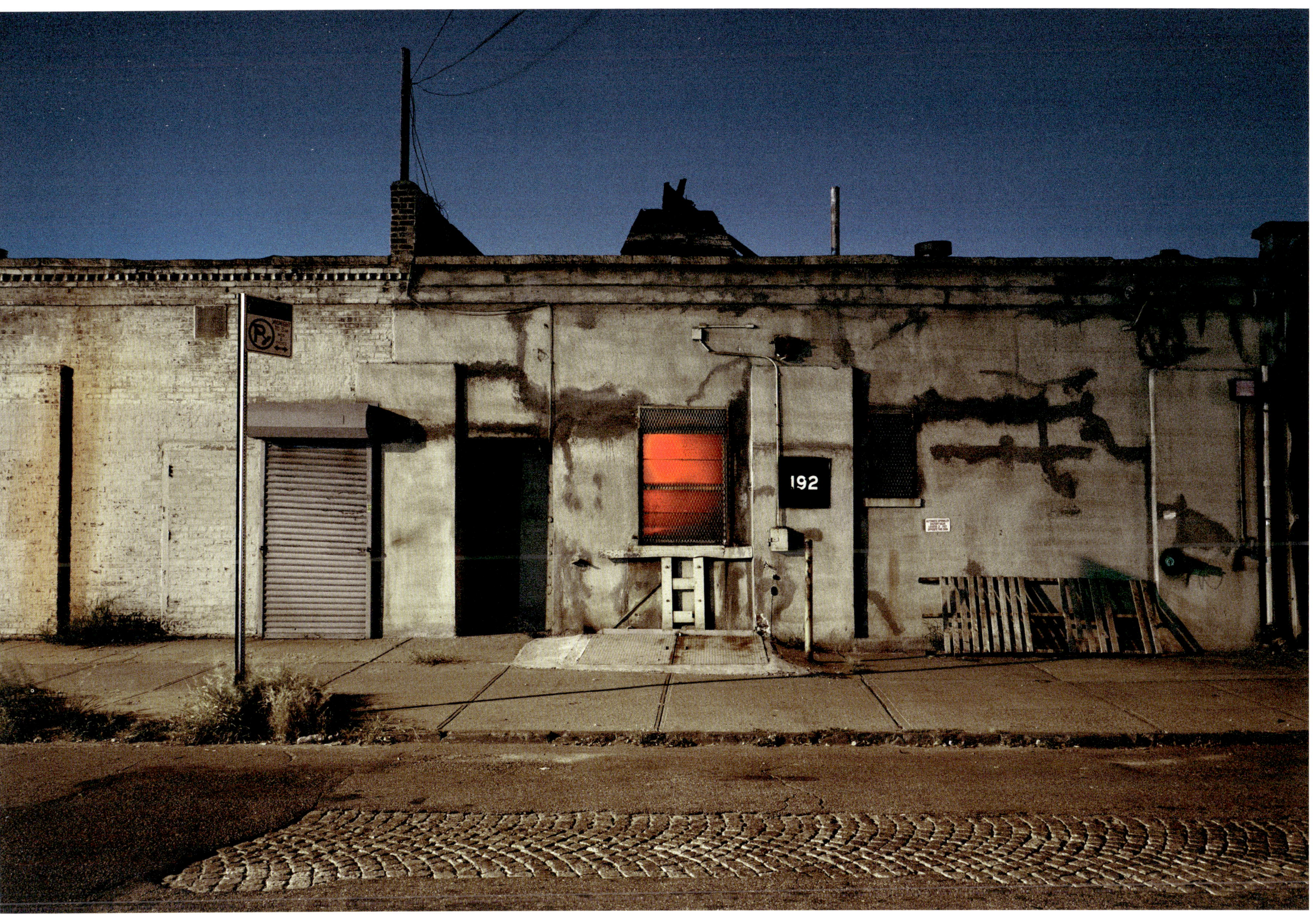
192

DARK CITY BY LYNN SAVILLE

I have been a roamer of limbo regions. These unloved and overlooked places are our last frontier. When I discover a site that attracts me, I return to it at dusk. In this liminal period, daylight gives way to moonlight and to the artificial light of streetlamps, advertisements, and surveillance.

Several years ago, I was lured back to the central areas of the city, where economic turmoil produced gaps in the urban façade—vacant stores whose glowing windows could resemble a Rothko painting. I began my series titled "Dark City" to pursue this contrast between aesthetic perception and the subtext of economic distress, a contrast that evoked a disquieting beauty. In effect, I was seeking to capture the ways in which urban places become spaces and vice versa. The photograph *Abandoned Michigan Central Depot, Detroit, Michigan*, for instance, shows a place that has become a looming shell of itself, a space.

Gradually, I became aware of a rhythm of transition in storefronts and empty lots that seemed to be part of an urban ecology and growth cycle. As the economy improved, shuttered stores were converted to new businesses. I came to appreciate that this process had its own iconography, whose symbols included the ladder and the broom. I also began to see how a scene first perceived as vacant had its own secret plenitude: a lively visual "conversation" among tools, abandoned objects, and reflections.

I captured such a conversation, for example, in *Marginal Street, New York City*. Looking into an empty restaurant at twilight, I was surprised to see what resembled an accidental art installation. The elements of this transient, random work included reflections of the New Jersey Palisades behind me, spectral highlights from a shiny doorframe, and a ladder positioned as if someone was ready to begin work on a rectangle of light.

The process of photographing empty storefronts—and, as I widened my focus, compromised ecosystems close to the city, like the Meadowlands in New Jersey; empty billboards, captured on the fly from trains and buses; untended lots; ghosted figures; and industrial sites—gave me an increasing sense of the richness of vacancy as a descriptor and a concept. It became for me not only a synonym for absence, but also a source of creative intrigue, in which signs of previous occupation, failure, and loss mingle with hints of renewal and re-creation. Such hints appear in *Brooklyn Bridge Park Construction*, taken on a restricted site where a park employee let me wander for an hour at twilight.

I continue to photograph cities at dawn or dusk, transitional times that underscore the shifting and multivalent nature of empty but evolving urban spaces. In addition, I have been working in cities other than New York—for example, Los Angeles, Portland (Maine), Boston, Cleveland, Detroit, and Houston—so that the series has a more national scope.

Finally, I have come to realize that in this series neither a city's iconic sites nor its goods are on display. This is perhaps unexpected, given that we often assume a city's purpose *is* display—of persons, commodities, architecture, and spectacles of all sorts. But for me, the dark city has been stripped of its agreed-upon attractions. It is an empty skeletal set in which objects can dream, and light and shadow can dance uninterrupted.

The Meadowlands, Secaucus, New Jersey

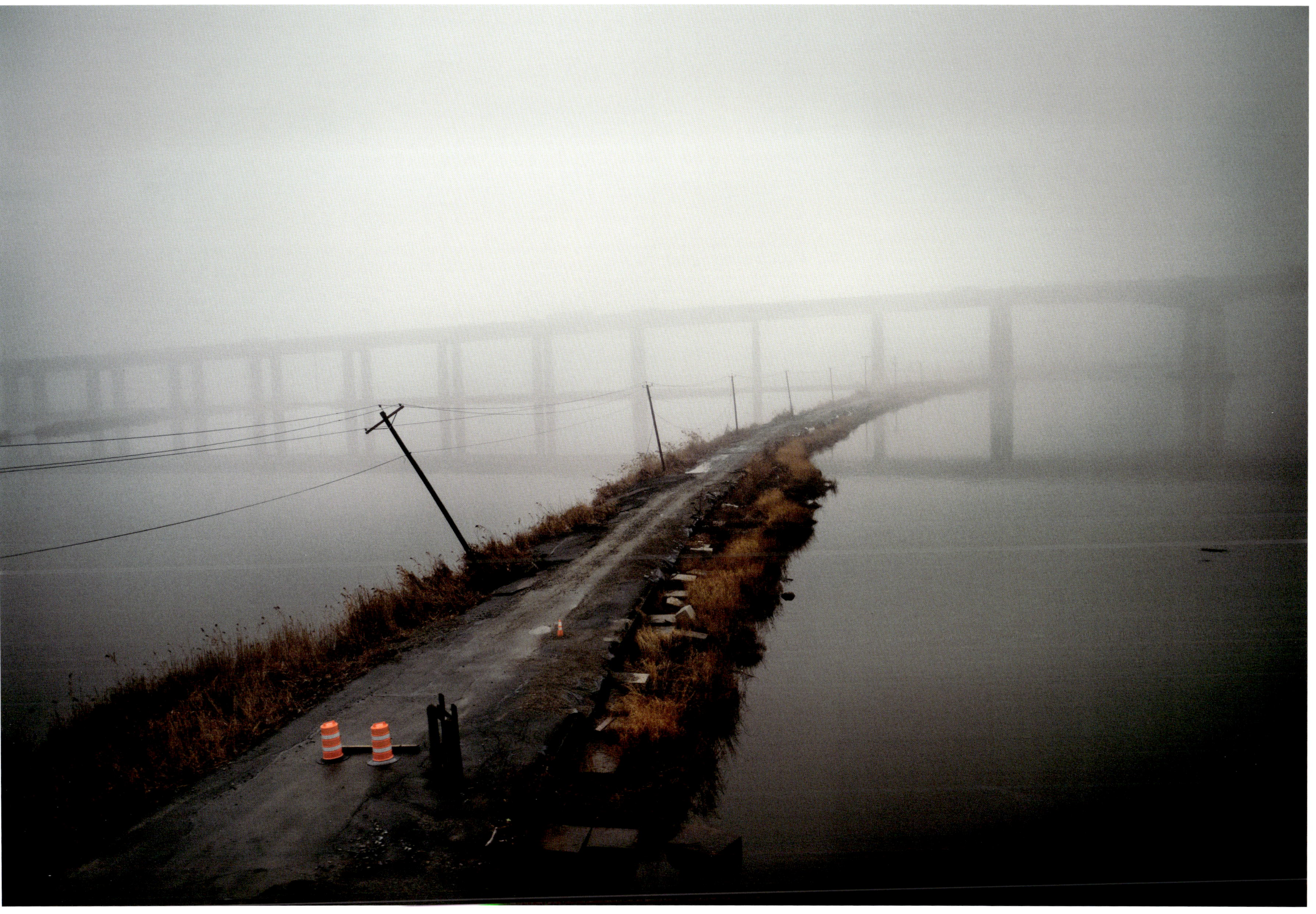

ACKNOWLEDGEMENTS

The pictures in this book were, for the most part, conceived as I worked alone in frequently deserted urban areas. As such, they invite readers, one at a time, into a mood of solitary contemplation. In another sense, however, the making of this book involved the work of many hands. It takes a village, apparently, to create scenes of solitude, and I would like to acknowledge all those who helped me place this book in your hands.

I'm grateful to my photography buddies Ken Fishman, James Gentile, David Kutz, Sam Oppenheim, and Steve Ronaghan, who occasionally accompanied me to isolated places, shared my enthusiasm, and kept a watchful eye. I'm also grateful to the urban guides who escorted me around various cities, giving me the freedom to look and dream: Don Pardee (Albany and Troy, New York), Mario Muller (Los Angeles), Daniel Seybold (Detroit), and Amber Cole (Seattle). Special thanks go to Albany artists Michael Conlin and William Butler of the collective Straight Crooked for permission to include my photograph of their mural, *This Is Happening in Your City Right Now!*

Pictures, even those conveying solitude, must fraternize in the society of a book. The internationally acclaimed designer Yolanda Cuomo, together with Bonnie Briant, her associate designer, have been essential in helping me create a book from a series of photographs. I am grateful to Jonno Rattman for applying his corrective magic to help nudge and coax these photographs into their final form. Similarly, Angel Cobos of Laumont Labs, Gerard Franciosa of My Own Color Lab, James Gentile, and Perri Hofmann have worked with expert care in scanning and preparing digital files.

I'm thrilled and honored to have my depictions of the *Dark City* published by Damiani Editore, whose high-quality production values are known and respected throughout the art world. Damiani director Andrea Albertini, who showed an immediate appreciation for this project, has helped make my dream of solitude into a real thing in the world.

Another dream realized was having Geoff Dyer, whose book *The Ongoing Moment* I so admire, write an introduction to *Dark City*. I'm grateful to him for his quirky and keen insights that help me better understand what I see.

Several institutions, and staff members associated with them, have played a key role in sustaining my work and deserve to be acknowledged. At Duke University, my alma mater, the David M. Rubenstein Rare Book and Manuscript Library has provided a permanent home for my archives. David Ferriero, then head of the Duke libraries and now Archivist of the United States, was instrumental in establishing that archive. I'm deeply grateful to him; to Deborah Jakubs, Rita DiGiallonardo Holloway University Librarian; to Robert Byrd, Associate University Librarian; and to the perceptive and talented curators I have had the pleasure of working with: Karen Glynn, Kirston Johnson, and Lisa McCarty. In addition, Duke professor Margaret Sartor, a superb photographer and writer, has been generous in giving her support and advice for this and other projects.

An institution I regard as my home away from home is New York City's International Center of Photography (ICP), where I have taught my course "New York at Twilight" for many years. I want to thank ICP's Philip S. Block, Deputy Director; Suzanne Nicholas, Associate Director of Education; and Deirdre Donohue, the Stephanie Shuman Librarian, for their warmth and readiness to share their ample knowledge of photography books. I am also grateful to my students, too many to name, who have accompanied me on twilight journeys around the city in rain, fog, snow, and other challenging conditions.

At New York University, another institution dear to me, Terry Shtob, Director of the Arts, Humanities, and Writing programs for NYU-SPS, has enthusiastically welcomed my teaching classes on photographing New York City.

Yancey Richardson, my longtime gallerist, has been generous in her support of my vision of the urban night landscape, as have Maggie Waterhouse, her Director of Sales, and Walker Waugh, her former Director. Other gallerists who deserve a special thanks are Arlette Kayafas (Boston) and Martha Schneider (Chicago).

Curators and critics who have provided advice and support include Carla Hanzal, Minny Lee, Lyle Rexer, Karen Sinsheimer, and Paul Wombell.

The comradeship of colleagues and friends has always been essential to my vision of twilight solitude. In that spirit, I offer my heartfelt thanks to Bill Armstrong, Beth Caspar, Meg Dooley, Hazel Kandall, Kay Kenny, Harsha Murthy, Margaret Neill, and Robert Schaefer.

My first lessons in night photography came from watching Lloyd and Curtis Saville, my father and brother, as they planned and carried out their imaginative projects. Eugenia Saville, my mother, inspired me by example as she pursued her career as a professor of music.

I'm ending with my husband, Philip Fried, but I could have begun with him as well—because he makes everything possible.

Lynn Saville
Dark City

Book Design by Yolanda Cuomo Design, NYC
Associate Designer: Bonnie Briant
Reproduction and Print Preparation: Jonno Rattman

DAMIANI

Damiani
Bologna, Italy
info@damianieditore.com
www.damianieditore.com

Printed in May 2015 by Grafiche Damiani - Faenza Group, Italy.

ISBN 978-88-6208-411-6